ALSO BY ANTHONY J. BADGER

New Deal/New South: An Anthony J. Badger Reader

The New Deal: The Depression Years 1933–1940

North Carolina and the New Deal

Prosperity Road: The New Deal, Tobacco, and North Carolina

FDR: The First Hundred Days

F D R:

The First Hundred Days

Anthony J. Badger

A Critical Issue
Consulting Editor: Eric Foner

Hill and Wang
A division of Farrar, Straus and Giroux
New York

Hill and Wang
A division of Farrar, Straus and Giroux
18 West 18th Street, New York 10011

Library of Congress Cataloging-in-Publication Data
Badger, Anthony J.
    FDR : the first hundred days / Anthony J. Badger.— 1st ed.
        p.   cm.
    Includes bibliographical references and index.
    ISBN-13: 978-0-8090-4441-2 (hardcover : alk. paper)
    ISBN-10: 0-8090-4441-2 (hardcover : alk. paper)
    1. New Deal, 1933–1939.   2. United States—Economic conditions—
1918–1945.   3. United States—Politics and government—1933–1945.
4. Roosevelt, Franklin D. (Franklin Delano), 1882–1945.   I. Title.

E806.B237 2008
973.917—dc22

                                                    2008004453

Designed by Jonathan D. Lippincott

www.fsgbooks.com

1   3   5   7   9   10   8   6   4   2

For
Bill Leuchtenburg
Jim Patterson
Dan Carter

Contents

Time Line

1932

July 2: Roosevelt flies to the Democratic National Convention in Chicago from Albany to deliver his acceptance speech in person.

November 8: FDR and the Democrats win the election by a landslide. Democrats take control of both houses of Congress.

November 22: Hoover meets FDR at the White House to discuss European debt repayment.

December 17: Hoover sends a telegram to FDR about the World Economic Conference.

1933

January 20: Hoover meets with FDR again about debt repayment.

February 14: The governor of Michigan declares a bank holiday.

February 15: FDR survives an assassination attempt in Miami.

February 18: Hoover's handwritten letter is delivered to FDR asking Roosevelt to commit to sound currency and a balanced budget.

March 4: The governors of Illinois and New York shut their banks. FDR is inaugurated the 32nd president of the United States.

March 5: FDR issues a proclamation declaring a four-day bank holiday throughout the nation effective March 6, and summons Congress to a special session for March 9.

March 8: FDR conducts his first presidential press conference.

March 9: Congress passes the Emergency Banking Act.

March 12: FDR gives his first "fireside chat."

March 13: Congress passes the Economy Act and amends the Volstead Act to legalize beer.

March 31: Congress passes the act establishing the Civilian Conservation Corps (CCC).

April 19: FDR takes the nation off the gold standard.

May 12: Congress passes the Federal Emergency Relief Act, and Roosevelt signs the Agricultural Adjustment Act.

May 18: Congress establishes the Tennessee Valley Authority (TVA).

May 27: Congress passes the Securities Act.

June 6: Congress passes the National Employment System Act.

June 13: Congress passes the Home Owners Refinancing Act.

June 16: Congress passes the National Industrial Recovery Act establishing the Public Works Administration (PWA) and the National Recovery Administration (NRA). Roosevelt also signs the Farm Credit Act, the Banking Act (which establishes FDIC), and the Railroad Coordination Act.

July 3: FDR sends his bombshell message to the World Economic Conference in London.

Introduction

In the week following Franklin D. Roosevelt's inauguration as president of the United States on March 4, 1933, more than 460,000 Americans wrote to him in the White House. This unprecedented personal communication from ordinary Americans continued. During the rest of his presidency an average of more than six thousand people a day wrote to him. Hoover had had one secretary to handle incoming correspondence that averaged six hundred letters a day. Roosevelt had to bring in fifty people to staff the White House mail room. The volume of correspondence generated led Roosevelt to conclude that neither the National Archives nor the Library of Congress could store this material in Washington. He proposed building a presidential library to house the documents of his presidency on his own estate at Hyde Park. He deeded the land to the federal government and raised the money from his friends and supporters to build the library. In return, Congress agreed to staff and administer it. FDR laid the cornerstone for his library on November 19, 1939. In his speech, he was at pains to highlight the letters of those ordinary Americans who had written to him over the previous six years when he said:

> Of the papers which will come to rest here, I personally attach less importance to the documents of those who have occupied high public or private office than I do the spontaneous letters which have come to me . . . from men, from

women, and from children in every part of the United States, telling me of their conditions and problems and giving me their own opinions.

Within two years of his death, his pre-presidential papers were open to scholars for study. By 1950, 85 percent of the Roosevelt papers had been cleared and could be used. In the battle for historical reputation, Roosevelt had defeated Herbert Hoover just as he had in the 1932 general election. It would not be until 1967 that historians could start scholarly work on the Hoover presidency, when his papers were made available at the Hoover Library, in West Branch, Iowa.

By establishing his library, Roosevelt transformed the keeping and status of presidential records. Before 1933 these papers were assumed to be the private property of the incumbents when they left office. Their preservation was haphazard: sometimes they ended up in the Library of Congress; often they remained in private hands or were destroyed. Presidents after Roosevelt have all raised private funds to establish ever grander presidential libraries, whose operation taxpayers fund.

Publicly, Roosevelt appeared modest and restrained about memorializing his presidency. He wanted no elaborate memorial in Washington. Instead, he requested a small marble slab, simply inscribed, to be placed outside the National Archives. In fact, Roosevelt was neither modest nor disinterested in shaping his historical legacy. He originally intended to screen all his correspondence personally before it could be transferred to his library. He anticipated three thousand visitors a week coming to the library and museum. What they would be interested in, he believed, was not the documentary record of his presidency but the artifacts of his life: everything that he had collected, from naval prints to stamps to books. He personally scaled down the reading area that would be set aside for scholars.

The mere existence of the library shaped the legacy Roosevelt bequeathed to his successors and historians in a substantive way. His plans perpetuated "the presidential synthesis" in which American history is seen largely through the lens of presidential administrations. Roosevelt left his successors a model of a dynamic, activist presidency that could not be ignored. All subsequent presidents, especially liberal Democrats, have labored "in the shadow of FDR." Their presidential accomplishments have been judged by the standards of the strong, charismatic national leadership that Roosevelt displayed in the fight, first, against the Great Depression, then against the Axis powers in World War II.

Nowhere was the standard set by Roosevelt more daunting for his successors than in his extraordinary achievements during his first hundred days in office.

Taking the reins of government on March 4, 1933, when the banks were closed and the nation paralyzed, Roosevelt warned Americans that, if Congress did not act decisively, he would ask it for "broad executive power to wage war against the emergency, as great as the power that would be given to me if we were in fact invaded by a foreign foe." That passage drew the most sustained applause of the day. The cantankerous Congress, which had been gridlocked in bitter recrimination with the outgoing president, responded enthusiastically to Roosevelt's patriotic appeals. Congressmen laid aside previous divisions, discarded long-held principles, and grasped, both for themselves and for the executive, vast, often unspecified, powers unheard of in peacetime. By June 16, after one hundred days of frenzied activity, sixteen pieces of major legislation gave the federal government the power to decide which banks should or should not reopen, to regulate the Stock Exchange, to determine the gold value of the dollar, to prescribe minimum wages and prices, to pay farmers not to produce, to pay money to the unemployed, to plan and regenerate a whole river basin across six states, to spend billions of dollars on public works, and to underwrite credit for bankers, homeowners, and farmers.

Presidents have been expected to follow FDR's lead. When in

1992 Bill Clinton was elected during a recession, it was predicted that he would "in his first hundred days . . . take a muscular Franklin Roosevelt–like approach to the slump." As Jimmy Carter's adviser Stuart Eizenstat noted, since FDR, "the first hundred days of an administration have been closely watched as a sign of what can be expected over the course of the entire administration." The first hundred days of the New Deal have served as a model for future presidents of bold leadership and executive-legislative harmony. Throughout his presidency, Lyndon B. Johnson consistently measured his record against that of his political hero, FDR. In April 1965 he pressed his congressional liaison man, Larry O'Brien, to "jerk out every damn little bill you can and get them down here by the 12th" because "on the 12th you'll have the best Hundred Days. Better than he did! . . . if you'll just put out that propaganda . . . that they've done more than they did in Roosevelt's Hundred Days."

Even if *The New York Times* was right on April 24, 1993, when it announced that "the hundred days test is, of course, fundamentally silly," most presidents have felt themselves held to account by it. Concerned that he would fail the test, Richard Nixon wrote in 1969, "In about five weeks we will have completed 100 days since the Inauguration. I would like to have this week a summary of the legislative proposals we have already sent to the Congress, and a hard analysis of what other legislative proposals will have been sent to the Congress for action before the 100 day period expires." He was certain that departments had not been working fast enough to meet this symbolic deadline. Aware that "after 100 days, the dam against criticism comes crashing down, and 80 days have gone by already," he and his staff created a "Hundred Days Group" and proposed a First Quarter Report that would "get off the hook on quantity of legislation being the first measure of success of the first 100 days." Even in 2006 the notion of a dynamic hundred days of legislative achievement was so beguiling that Speaker-elect Nancy Pelosi in November promised that the new

Democratic majority would enact major parts of what it had promised in the midterm campaign, not merely in a hundred days, but in a hundred hours.

Yet, as Arthur Schlesinger, the masterful narrator of the New Deal, observed, there was a hundred days "trap." Roosevelt's Hundred Days was a "unique episode which grew out of a unique crisis." My first aim in this book is to analyze what was unique about the success of the first hundred days. There were very particular circumstances that enabled Roosevelt, but not subsequent presidents, to exercise such bold leadership and to command such widespread congressional support during that period.

But what did this legislation achieve?

For Bill Clinton's grandfather, Roosevelt brought economic salvation so that when he died he expected to "go to Roosevelt." In the words of one liberal historian, for many Americans "something magical" happened in the Hundred Days. For the first time the federal government took responsibility for the economic welfare of ordinary Americans who had felt helpless in the face of economic catastrophe. For Jonathan Alter in 2006, the Hundred Days was a defining moment that created a new America with a new sense of social obligation, "a country of commitment to one another." Alter told "a story of how at one of the darkest moments in American political history, a political and communicative genius saved American democracy."

But that celebration of the Hundred Days and the subsequent New Deal has been challenged.

Critics on the right, ranging from Herbert Hoover to economic historians of the 1980s and 1990s, have argued that Roosevelt artificially created a crisis in 1933, used the analogy of the wartime emergency, and foisted economic regimentation and government control onto the American people. For them, 1933 was a decisive wrong turn in American history, one that set the nation firmly on the road to collectivism and the creation of a Leviathan that is the modern insatiable, bureaucratic state. As a result, conservative critics argue, the commitment of both ordinary Americans and their leaders to individualism, the free market, and limited government suffered a blow from which the nation has never fully recovered. For Amity Shlaes, writing in 2007, Calvin Coolidge and Andrew Mellon were the heroes of interwar America; the villains were Herbert Hoover and Franklin Roosevelt, who both failed because of their penchant for government intervention and their lack of faith in the marketplace.

Critics on the left, ranging from Communists in 1933 to the New Left in the 1960s to historians in the 1990s writing on business leaders, have argued that there had never been a better time than the Hundred Days for the radical overhaul of the American economic and political system. The capitalist system had collapsed, and American workers and farmers were more disillusioned than ever before, or since, with traditional business leadership. For once, leaders of corporate capitalism could not solve their problems through economic expansion overseas, since there were no foreign markets to exploit. The alternative, they feared, was a radical redistribution of both wealth and power at home. To forestall that change, corporate leaders, radical critics argue, were the driving force behind the Hundred Days, patching up rather than tearing down the old economic system. They ensured that power remained largely in the hands of traditional leaders, and they defused by the most minimal measures possible the angry discontent of the poor. According to this argument, business interests were paramount in the formulation of public policy, and the New Deal was "part and parcel of two decades of business strategy and . . . business-driven recovery politics."

My second aim is to assess the nature of the changes that the Hundred Days brought and to identify the driving forces behind them. The newly acquired powers of government in 1933 were important, but precisely circumscribed. Corporate leaders were only one, and not even the most powerful, group among a number of policy players. In 1933 the capacity of the American state for economic intervention was minimal. The circumstances of the all-too-real economic emergency in 1933 dictated that the New Deal response rely on speed, voluntarism, and consent. Compulsion, the acquisition by the state of the means of production, central overhead planning, and redistributive taxation were never a possibility.

Some of the prominent figures of the Hundred Days—Harry Hopkins, Henry Wallace, and Harold Ickes—would still be central figures in the government when FDR died in 1945. Others who survived, such as Henry Morgenthau, Jr., and Frances Perkins, played relatively minor roles in the early months of the administration. Some key players in the Hundred Days, by contrast, would pass quickly from the stage or the good graces of the administration. Men such as the Brains Truster Raymond Moley; Lewis Douglas, advocate of a rigid economy; Hugh Johnson and George Peek, the protégés of Bernard Baruch; and Wilsonian warhorse Dan Roper were influential in 1933 but played little role afterward.

My third aim is therefore to identify how important the legislation of the Hundred Days was for the longer-term phenomenon of New Deal liberalism. Relief for the unemployed, the protection of labor standards, farm price supports, and public works spending were all part of the Hundred Days. But so were measures designed to slash government spending, foster business-government cooperation, and increase the tax burden through regressive excise taxes. It was by no means inevitable at the end of the Hundred Days that the former would be the shape of the New Deal future while the latter became redundant.

Roosevelt famously assured the American people in his inaugural that they had "nothing to fear but fear itself." In fact, Americans had every reason to be fearful. When Roosevelt took office in March 1933, even the prospects for the survival of democracy itself looked bleak. Hitler had come to power in Germany, and totalitarianism was dominant in Italy, Russia, and Japan. Democratic governments across Europe were fragile and unpopular. With the future of capitalism and democracy at stake, Roosevelt responded with unprecedented vigor and elicited a remarkable popular response. This book aims to explain how a president could act so boldly and attract such popular backing, to assess what that bold leadership achieved, and to see how much of the permanent and lasting imprint of the New Deal could be discerned in those first hundred days.

FDR: *The First Hundred Days*

ONE

The Problem and the Players

The Great Depression

Americans had never been there before. On March 4, 1933, the nation's banks had been closed. At least a quarter, but more likely a third, of American workers were unemployed. Those fortunate enough to have work had seen their income fall by a third in three years. Farmers had been crushed by catastrophic price falls, drought, and debt. A thousand homeowners a day were losing their homes. No region, no industry, no class escaped the Depression. In no other Western industrialized nation was the impact of the Depression so pervasive.

Yet in the 1920s Americans had enjoyed unprecedented prosperity that had brought the nation, as presidential candidate Herbert Hoover had proclaimed in 1928, "nearer to the final triumph over poverty than ever before." The American genius for innovation and efficiency had manufactured immense gains in productivity that were the marvel of the rest of the world. High wages, abundant resources, and technological advances created what could be described as a consumer society in which many Americans could afford to think beyond the demands of immediate subsistence for the first time and contemplate new standards of domestic comfort. They purchased cars and bought their own homes, wiring them for electricity to install appliances ranging from irons to radios to washing machines. Many were able to invest in a stock market that climbed relentlessly and seemed to promise unlimited and certain riches.

America was also the linchpin of the world economy. Before World War I the United States had been a debtor nation, with its economic expansion funded by European investors. But America had funded the Allied war effort and emerged in 1918 as the leading creditor nation in the world: its financial institutions, awash with funds, primed European and Latin American economic recovery, and its government chipped away at the war debts incurred by the Allies.

Before 1914, world trade flourished under the economic stability of the gold standard, presided over by Britain, France, and Germany: a world in which exchange rates were fixed and where currencies could be converted into gold on demand. In the relatively well-insulated prewar political climate, few doubted that every country would strive to exercise the necessary financial discipline and stay on gold. When currencies were threatened, central bankers in London, Paris, and Berlin would cooperate to mount rescue operations. It took time to restore the gold standard after the war. With Britain and France off the gold standard until 1926, the dollar was now the key reserve currency, and New York, not London, was the dominant international financial center. The United States had one third of the world's gold reserves. Throughout the 1920s the Federal Reserve Board kept interest rates low as it sought to ease the British return to the gold standard and prevent devaluation in Europe. American wealth not only served as a model and source of wonder to other nations, but also seemed to be financing their economic success.

But flaws in the structure of both the domestic and international economy made that prosperity difficult to sustain. American farmers saw little of the good times of the 1920s. They had gone into debt to expand production when European farms were ravaged by war: they now had surplus capacity as European agriculture revived, and their debts were an even greater burden as world commodity prices fell. Overcapacity was also the story throughout the twenties for major traditional employers—coal, textiles, and railroads—who attempted to fight off the competition of new fuels, fibers, and modes of transport by expanding production, cutting prices, and slashing labor costs. In 1930, 60 percent of American families received less than $2,000 a year and therefore lived below the subsistence standard as calculated by the Brookings Institution. Sharecroppers, migrant workers, African Americans, Native Americans, widows, and the elderly remained mired in poverty.

The new industries that led the way to prosperity in the 1920s— the technologically advanced consumer durable industries that manufactured automobiles and electrical goods—could not entirely compensate for this lack of consumer purchasing power. They simply did not yet constitute a large enough sector of the economy. Wages may have been high by international standards, urban population growth may have been impressive, but employment was often irregular, and neither the wage levels nor the new jobs could absorb the surplus rural population or create the consumer demand necessary to sustain the production levels of the new industries or of the heavy industry, like steel, that supplied them.

An inevitable economic slowdown—in which employers cut both jobs and wages, thereby taking even more purchasing power out of the economy and stimulating further wage and job cuts in a downward deflationary spiral—was foreshadowed by a slowdown in the construction industry. Cyclical recessions were, by definition, familiar. What turned a slowdown into the worst depression in American history was the weakness not only of the American financial system but also of world financial structures. The crisis in the "nervous system of capitalism" precipitated the most significant international economic collapse of the twentieth century.

Even in the prosperous twenties the fragility of the U.S. banking system was exposed. All too often small rural banks could not withstand the demands made on their limited resources during routine economic fluctuations. Urban banks that attempted to come to their rescue found themselves under pressure as so many of their own assets, either in property or in securities, were rendered worthless and frightened depositors withdrew their holdings, squeezing even more purchasing power out of the economy. As a result, banks found many of their assets tied up in bankrupt railroads and repossessed farms and homes.

The banks had encouraged speculation on the stock market, purchasing securities rather than municipal bonds and lending money for stock market speculation rather than for commercial development. Stock market speculation was further encouraged by the cheap money policies of the Federal Reserve, which did not tighten its controls until 1928. Inadequately regulated, the stock market crashed in October 1929. The initial crash was no mere technical correction nor a mere elimination of overvalued stock: more and more investors sold, prompting further falls in share prices, which increasingly reflected the depressed performance of the economy as a whole. In the long run $85 billion in share values were wiped out.

The gold standard ceased to promote economic stability as it had before the war. Countries relying predominantly on agriculture saw their export earnings plummet as commodity prices slumped. Faced with balance-of-payment deficits, they were forced to devalue their currency.

The European industrialized nations struggled to rebuild their economies and keep their traditional industries competitive. It was difficult to maintain financial discipline when newly empowered workers demanded government action to assist the unemployed and interest groups resisted new taxation. International cooperation was difficult. Rearmament provoked political conflict. Germany and Austria protested the level of their reparation payments to the victorious Allies. The Allies in turn complained of the demands of repaying war debts to the Americans. When the stock market crashed in 1929, the gold standard, far from stabilizing the international economy, in fact exported financial instability to Europe, as Barry Eichengreen has demonstrated. The Federal Reserve decision to raise interest rates in 1928 not only restricted much-needed commercial credit in the United States when the economic downturn started but also dried up American loans to Germany and Austria. These loans had facilitated German and Austrian payment of reparations. In 1931, German and Austrian banks buckled under these pressures of reparation demands, loan repayments, and social unrest. A British-inspired rescue package merely exposed the extent to which British assets were tied up in Germany and led to a run on the pound. The British government devalued its currency, left the gold standard, and raised its tariffs. American banks now had assets frozen in central Europe. As tariff barriers, including America's own, were raised, world trade contracted further. As major countries devalued their currencies, speculators turned their attention to America's gold reserves and attacked the dollar. Thus, the already fragile American financial system was put under even further strain.

The Response

American leaders had only the feeblest of governmental weapons available to them to attack this economic disaster. The United States in the 1920s, observed William E. Leuchtenburg, "had almost no institutional structure to which Europeans would accord the term 'the State.'" Washington, commented one contemporary, was "a sleepy, rather inconsequential Southern town that nobody would have thought of calling the center of anything important. For most citizens their only contact with the federal government was the post office." Under Calvin Coolidge, half the employees of the federal government were in the Post Office. The government raised and spent relatively small sums of money. In fiscal year 1930, federal spending amounted to only 3.5 percent of gross national product. Most of the time before the 1930s, except during war, the government lived within its means: over two thirds of budgets before 1933 were balanced. Revenue was raised through indirect excise taxes and tariff duties on imports. Only 5 percent of Americans paid income tax. In 1929, federal tax receipts were only 3.8 percent of gross national product (to emphasize the context, the figure for 1981 was 20.1 percent).

The government had few tools with which to macromanage the economy. The United States had had a central bank only since 1914. Federal Reserve Board officials, notably the powerful governor of the New York Federal Reserve, controlled interest rates and the money supply. New York and Washington Reserve bankers did not speak with one voice: they differed notably about the wisdom of international cooperation. The public works programs of the federal government paled into insignificance beside public construction by the state and local governments or the construction levels of private industry.

Nor did the federal government have the tools with which to micromanage the economy. The government lacked even the most basic statistical information about the economy. Its estimates of the number of unemployed were, at best, extrapolations from amateurish estimates and surveys. It would not be until the implementation of the Social Security Act in 1935 that the government could make reasonably confident statements on unemployment. As far as caring for the unemployed and the needy, the United States was an "awkward outlier," a "welfare laggard" compared with the industrialized and urbanized countries of Western Europe. It provided no unemployment insurance, no old-age pension or assistance to the needy aged, and no relief to the unemployed, who were left to the tender mercies of private charity and the localities and states. The great welfare spending program of the federal government in the past, the payment of pensions to Civil War veterans (in the South, provided by state governments to Confederate veterans), had not been the starting point for a more generous provision to all the aged.

If Americans looked to their own history, they had two precedents to turn to in this crisis. The country's worst economic crisis had previously been in 1893–1894. As in 1933, a president was faced with armies of the unemployed, desperate farmers, and frightened financiers. President Grover Cleveland had resolutely maintained a policy of sound money and strict economy. He had steadfastly resisted demands for federal government assistance. His courage won him the praise of conservatives everywhere but split his Democratic Party, brought it electoral disaster, and condemned the party to national minority status for a generation.

In 1917, America had to mobilize men and resources to fight a European war. The federal government exercised vast emergency powers, drafted men, set farm prices, allocated scarce materials, and spent billions of dollars to fund war production. The American economy clearly had capacities that few had previously contemplated that could be unlocked by government intervention. Some economists saw a possible peacetime role for the government in promoting economic efficiency and also in stabilizing cyclical economic fluctuations. These economists were also drawing on twenty years of debate by progressive reformers and social scientists about the nature of unemployment. They had come to recognize that unemployment in an industrial society was not the result of laziness or individual failings. The government could act to alleviate distress, and should attempt to find out just how many people were unemployed. A system of labor exchanges could match unemployed workers to available jobs, as the United States Employment Service had done with some success in 1918. Schemes of unemployment insurance would provide incentives for employers to keep workers on. Bringing forward public works spending could make up for a shortfall in construction activity and thus lessen the impact of any economic downturn. As Udo Sautter has observed, by 1918, "virtually all the major tools that later found application in governmental unemployment action were designed and discussed."

Economic orthodoxy remained strong then and throughout the 1920s. Bankers strove to maintain the international gold standard. The fiscal discipline dictated by the gold standard mandated a balanced budget, and few bankers or businessmen dissented from the need to avoid budget deficits. During the 1920s, budget surpluses enabled the Republicans to cut taxes. After three years of depression, in June 1932 the overwhelming majority of bank presidents still favored a balanced budget. The gold standard orthodoxy demanded free trade, but there Republicans dissented. The Fordney-McCumber and the Smoot-Hawley tariffs produced record tariff levels, despite the outrage of academic economists. Republicans justified them as a way of protecting the high wages of American workers.

But the Republican president who first confronted the Great Depression was not a prisoner of economic orthodoxy. Herbert Hoover was superbly qualified to lead the country at a time of economic crisis. He was intellectually at least the equal of any twentieth-century president. A highly successful businessman and engineer, he had achieved an international reputation as a public servant and Quaker humanitarian. He organized relief supplies to the Belgians during World War I, America's food production after the United States entered the war, and Russian famine relief afterward. Courted by both national political parties (and by a young Franklin Roosevelt), Hoover was the one dynamic presence in the Republican administrations of Harding and Coolidge. Restlessly progressive, as secretary of commerce he interfered in all aspects of the federal government, which he sought to streamline and make an expert and effective promoter of economic growth at home and overseas. He masterminded the government's apparently successful campaign to alleviate the 1920–1921 recession as he coordinated private and local relief activities and public works spending. He was no rigid laissez-faire ideologue. It was not the austere model of Grover Cleveland that Hoover turned to in 1929 but the model of his own intervention in 1921.

Hoover believed that what was distinctive about the American brand of individualism was the capacity of Americans for collective voluntary action. His role as president, as it had been as a wartime relief administrator and as recovery czar in 1921, was to draw on and encourage this willingness of individuals and groups to collaborate for the common good. He called businessmen together and challenged them to keep wages and prices up. He asked bankers to pool reserves to protect their weaker institutions. He encouraged farmers to form cooperatives, cut costs, and keep surplus crops off the market. He brought forward federal public works schemes and asked state governors to do the same. He called on the generosity of the American people and coordinated the efforts of private charities and local governments to provide assistance to the unemployed. It was a remarkable and imaginative rescue operation, and by the spring of 1930 Hoover would boast that for the first time in American history the general economy had been successfully quarantined from the impact of a stock market crash.

But Hoover's voluntarism, which could cope with a temporary recession in 1920–1921, could not cope with such a fundamental economic collapse ten years later. The deflationary pressure was too relentless. There would always be employers who felt they could capture a competitive edge with a wage and price cut. Even if wages were kept up by large corporations like U.S. Steel, such companies could not maintain employment levels and would eventually slash wages too. No farmer would cut back production if there was no guarantee that his neighbor would do likewise. Bankers did not offer to share risks to protect other banks; they kept everything they could to protect themselves. Public works investment was brought forward, but although construction volume held up in 1930 and 1931, it slumped in 1932. The sheer scale of unemployment soon exhausted the resources of private charity. As the Archdiocese of Chicago explained, "charity cannot and should not be expected to meet the terrific strain . . . It was never

meant to aid the majority." Local authorities could not raise sufficient revenue to take up the slack: their own revenue from property taxes was shrinking. Rural-dominated state legislatures, also
facing tax revolts from desperate property owners, were in no position to cope on a sufficient scale.

Hoover would not acknowledge that voluntarism had failed.
Instead, he argued that the United States had been well on its way
to recovery when the European financial collapse of 1931 negated
all his hard work. He therefore sought an international remedy. In
1931 he worked out a moratorium on debt repayments from the
Allies to the United States and on reparation payments from Germany to the Allies. He hoped to use a settlement of the question
of the Allies' debt to the United States as a lever to secure concessions from other governments on monetary stabilization and
tariffs: to end the competitive round of devaluation and tariff protection that choked off world trade. He believed that he was suc-
ceeding in restoring business confidence when confidence was
eroded by wild Democratic spending plans in Congress. Later,
confidence was further set back by business fears of the radicalism
of Democratic presidential candidate Franklin Roosevelt.

Hoover set his face firmly against coercive state action, although the distinction between un-American coercion and action
he considered legitimate often appeared arbitrary. He had encouraged trade associations, which shared information that enabled
firms not to engage in unnecessary competition and to keep labor
standards up. But when trade association leaders strove to formal-
ize such arrangements and seek exemption from the antitrust acts,
Hoover denounced such proposals as fascistic. He had always advocated public works spending as a means of correcting economic
downswings, but in 1932 he denounced programs for large-scale
spending. He was comfortable with his own budget deficits—
which would be eliminated when recovery came and tax revenues
returned—but by 1932 he regarded a balanced budget as an over-

riding priority, an indispensable component of an international settlement based on the gold standard.

As a result, Hoover acquiesced in more activist, interventionist domestic polices only with ill grace and in the face of irresistible political pressure in Congress. When bankers failed to cooperate in pooling resources in a National Credit Corporation, Hoover reluctantly agreed to the creation of the Reconstruction Finance Corporation, which could bail out threatened banks and railroads. As pressure grew for direct federal spending on relief, Hoover finally acquiesced in the Emergency Relief and Construction Act, which lent money to the states for relief spending and public works programs. After his electoral defeat, in the long interregnum between the November election and March inauguration, he attempted to tie Roosevelt into his international recovery program. He tried to get him to link the settlements of the war debts issue to the plan for the World Economic Conference, in the summer of 1933, which was to seek international agreement on a recovery program. Then he attempted to persuade Roosevelt to commit his incoming administration to a policy of sound money and a balanced budget. Hoover never lost his conviction that he had pursued the right policies but had been undermined by irresponsible and demagogic politicians, the most irresponsible of whom was Franklin D. Roosevelt.

FDR

Franklin D. Roosevelt had the most privileged background of any twentieth-century president. The only, and adored, child of landed New York parents, he was educated at private school and Harvard. Cushioned by his family money, he made little more than a desultory attempt to earn a living as a lawyer and in business. Instead, he went into state politics, fortunate to run for office in his Republican home district in a Democratic year, 1910. A patrician reformer, he alienated the most powerful figures in the state party, but his political career was rescued by the invitation to be assistant secretary of the navy in the Wilson administration. Roosevelt cut a dashing, if lightweight, figure in Wilsonian Washington. "He's really a beautiful looking man," said James Warburg's mother, "but he's so dumb." Roosevelt recklessly curried favor with the admirals, undercutting his much wiser but tolerant boss, Josephus Daniels, veteran North Carolina newspaperman. In 1914 he allowed himself to be talked into carrying the reform banner in a race for the U.S. Senate in New York, where he was crushed by the urban bosses. An affair with his secretary, Lucy Mercer, almost ended his political career and his marriage. The relationship with his wife, Eleanor, niece of Theodore Roosevelt, was never again physically intimate, and she determined to create a life for herself in her own right. In 1920 Franklin Roosevelt recaptured some credit from the New York party brokers by enthusiastically throwing himself into a forlorn race as vice presidential candidate.

In 1921 he was struck down by polio. Despite valiant efforts at recovery, hours spent at Warm Springs, Georgia, where he funded a polio institute, and his constant upbeat assessment of his progress, his condition improved little. Biographers, rehabilitation experts, and fellow polio victims have documented just how crippled Roosevelt was. But a "splendid deception" involving the willing collaboration of the media ensured that neither film nor photographic evidence allowed the American people to know the true extent of his disability. Few Americans then, or later, when he was president, knew that he was so wheelchair bound he had to be lifted like a baby to many locations. As Geoffrey Ward has pointed out, Roosevelt was "the most photographed and filmed American of his time." Yet only three photographs of him in his wheelchair survive, and less than a minute and a half of a sixteen-millimeter home movie demonstrates the excruciatingly painful and ungainly way he walked, on the arm of a bodyguard and with a cane. As

Ward notes, Roosevelt's "polished skill at duplicity, his positive delight in secrecy, in knowing things that others didn't . . . now superbly served his purposes."

That deviousness, masking of true intentions, and relishing of secrecy became almost a reflex reaction on Roosevelt's part. Yet polio revealed great depths of resilience on the part of a privileged young man who had rarely been denied whatever he wanted. If Roosevelt felt sorry for himself, he never allowed his self-pity to show. Veteran columnist Mary McGrory contrasted that reserve with the 1990s obsession with the politics of the personal and the confessional.

> He never, unlike nineties politicians, asked for pity. Today's leaders extort pity. They take us into boyhood homes and dreadful scenes with stepfathers, to the intensive care unit to visit a grievously injured child or to the deathbed of a sister. All such talk was unthinkable to Roosevelt. He bore his infirmities without complaint. Reserve was bred into him. He was a miracle of a man.

What went with Roosevelt's reserve was an easy charm that aroused the loyalty of people around him. From the time he acquired the assistance of Louis Howe, a gnarled New York reporter, to help him with his reelection bid in 1912, he had been able to identify and enlist people who would give him selfless and capable service. Yet the people around him needed Roosevelt more than he needed them. They never got too close to the private Roosevelt. They might have thought themselves indispensable, but each confidant in turn discovered he was not.

Polio made Eleanor Roosevelt an indispensable part of Roosevelt's political team. She had already started to carve out an independent life for herself, but with her husband incapacitated, she began to make speeches for him and to be his eyes and ears in state politics, and later in government. As part of a network of reform-minded women in New York politics, she was a powerful voice for social reform issues and a point of entry for Democratic women into the Roosevelt circle.

Polio also enabled Roosevelt to avoid the worst of the internecine ethnocultural battles that split the Democratic Party in the 1920s. Roosevelt cultivated progressive southern and western forces in the Democratic Party, exploiting the contacts he had made in the Wilson administration and during his vice presidential campaign. But he also memorably put the name of the hero of the northern urban immigrants, Al Smith, in nomination at the 1924 and 1928 national conventions. Smith, anxious for a strong gubernatorial candidate to help his ticket in New York in 1928, persuaded a cautious Roosevelt to run. Roosevelt's luck held. A narrow victory in New York in 1928, made possible by upstate, rural votes, suddenly became a launching pad for the presidency. When the Depression hit, Roosevelt won a landslide reelection victory in 1930.

Roosevelt's upstate New York upbringing and his links in the South and West gave a clue to his progressivism in the 1920s. He had always supported an activist role for government on behalf of the disadvantaged. He advocated with some passion the conservation of natural resources and the public development of electric power. From the start of the Depression he asserted that farmers needed help if recovery was to come. He had a patrician distaste for corruption and a personal contempt for business and financial leaders who had betrayed their fiduciary trust. As governor, he showed greater awareness than most state governors of the need for vigorous action to combat the Depression. New York was one of the few states to appropriate money for unemployment relief, and its program far outstripped that of other states in its scale and professionalism.

Nevertheless, Roosevelt's actions scarcely suggested that he appreciated the magnitude of the action needed to put the country on the road to recovery. He had shown no special insight into the state of the economy in the 1920s: he had been as caught up in the speculative boom as anybody. He seemed to possess utterly conventional notions of government finance and was reluctant to envisage large-scale public works spending. But he was a very attractive candidate to a Democratic Party that had been so divided between the rural South and West on the one hand, and the urban North on the other. The popular governor of a major industrial state, he did not alienate the southern and western political organizations in the way that the stridently "Wet," Catholic Al Smith had. Roosevelt stressed "Bread, not Booze": the economy was more important than the issue of Prohibition.

The need to get a two-thirds vote at the Democratic National Convention to secure the nomination always made a front-runner vulnerable. Roosevelt's most powerful and determined opponent was Al Smith himself. Some saw Smith as an embittered man, resentful of the lack of attention that his former protégé had paid to him and his advisers in Albany. But Smith's candidacy, backed by the urban city machine bosses and the powerful anti-Prohibitionist businessmen and National Committee officers John Raskob and Jouett Shouse, represented a genuinely conservative anti-statist opposition to a politician who they felt was entirely too comfortable with an activist government. Businessmen who opposed Prohibition hoped that repeal would ease their tax burden by providing an alternative source of revenue through excise taxes on alcohol. But they also viewed Prohibition as a gigantic measure of confiscation of a legitimate business and a symbol of government intervention they hated. Urban bosses wanted patronage, but they had entirely conventional notions of the role of government. Smith himself was more a business progressive than a welfare liberal. His denunciation of Roosevelt's speech that promised to aid "the forgotten man" sprang not from a newly minted friendship with rich businessmen but from genuine outrage at what he saw as a demagogic appeal to class bitterness. Raskob attempted to put together an alliance of conservative northeasterners who backed Smith and conservative southerners who backed the frugal Harry Byrd of Virginia. The aim of the alliance was to stop Roosevelt.

That campaign succeeded in denying Roosevelt victory on the first three ballots at the Chicago convention in 1932. Roosevelt's advisers, Jim Farley and Louis Howe, inexperienced on the national stage, failed to head off the candidacies of Smith and House speaker John Nance Garner of Texas. Roosevelt's bid was on the verge of failure when Garner released his supporters to back Roosevelt. Garner's realism and party loyalty, combined with the enduring anti-Smith bitterness of William Gibbs McAdoo, Jr., and the California delegation, enabled Roosevelt to be nominated. The narrowness of FDR's victory, and the nature of the opposition, are salutary reminders that the alternatives to Roosevelt were to the right, not the left. It is difficult to imagine the Hundred Days or the New Deal if Garner, Smith, Newton Baker, or the hopeful favorite sons had been elected—candidates whose vision scarcely reached past the repeal of Prohibition and economy in government.

The Victorious Roosevelt

Roosevelt broke with precedent and flew to Chicago to accept the nomination in person, rewarded Garner with the vice presidential nomination, and electrified the convention with a call for a New Deal for the American people. He then campaigned vigorously across the country to put any doubts about his health and physical condition to rest. The election returns in November could be seen as heralding a new party system where the Democrats were the national majority party. Political scientists dispute whether Roosevelt won by mobilizing new voters (women and immigrants), by building on the "Al Smith revolution" among urban lower-income voters, or by converting disaffected Republicans. The realignment would not be complete until 1936, but for the most part the voters of the West and the South gave Roosevelt electoral victory as they had given him the nomination.

Neither the election itself nor Roosevelt's actions during the interregnum between his victory in November and his inauguration in March made clear what specific policies Americans could expect from their new president.

Roosevelt, though no intellectual himself, was always willing to listen to experts. He was open-minded enough to admit his own ignorance and to absorb, often haphazardly, new ideas and information, not from books but through conversation with an unusually wide range of advisers. Conscious of his own, and his closest aides', lack of knowledge on national issues, he assembled in March 1932 a Brains Trust, comprising Columbia University academics, to explain the Depression and possible remedies.

Raymond Moley, a political scientist specializing in criminal justice reform; Rexford Tugwell, an institutional economist; and Adolf Berle, a legal financial expert on business structures, gave Roosevelt an analysis of the Depression diametrically opposed to Hoover's. None of them believed that traditional economic theory corresponded to the reality of American economic experience. Nor did they believe the Depression to be international in origin. It would take more than an international settlement of debts, trade, and exchange rates to solve America's problems, since those problems were the result of basic structural flaws in the domestic economy. There was a fundamental maldistribution of income that had led to a crucial lack of consumer purchasing power. To enable Americans to consume what they had the capacity to produce, policies had to be devised to raise farm income, increase wages, and make industrial prices less rigid. What was needed was a realistic acceptance of the structure of the American economy as it actually, rather than theoretically, existed. In particular, policy makers had to accept that, like it or not, large corporations and concentrations of economic power were there to stay in the modern economy. To break up monopolies and denounce speculators and financiers might have been the standard cry of many progressive politicians, but the Brains Trusters believed such battle cries had little relevance in bringing about the rational and effective organization of the economy.

The policy prescriptions of the Brains Trust were less clear. On the central issue of how to manage industry, they differed among themselves over the degree of coercion and central planning that might be either desirable or feasible. They were certain that there would have to be programs to restore the purchasing power of farmers, to assist the unemployed, and to ease the crippling burden of debt that tied up the assets of railroads, homeowners, and farmers. Roosevelt allowed little of their comprehensive vision to surface during the campaign. He seemed to take on board their underconsumptionist arguments, but his campaign only hinted at measures of planning and business self-regulation. He came out in favor of a farm plan but outlined only broad, all-embracing principles. He straddled the issue of the tariff and made one of his clearest commitments to cut government expenditure by 25 percent.

Roosevelt's desire to display impeccable fiscally responsible credentials reflected his own conventional economic beliefs and his need to reassure the conservative, business-oriented wing of his party. The more unequivocal policy prescriptions of the Brains Trust struggled to gain acceptance even after the election had been safely won. During the interregnum, Moley became the chief organizer of the president-elect's policy initiatives. He played a key role in preventing FDR from being sucked into commitments to the internationalist remedies outlined by Hoover. But Moley's portfolio was so vast that he could make relatively little specific policy input. Tugwell attracted unwanted publicity for his more radical ideas. He did succeed, however, in selling the domestic allotment plan, a voluntary production-control measure, to both Roosevelt and the farm leaders, and the plan became the central plank of New Deal farm policy. But even in farm policy he found himself competing with Roosevelt's old friend Henry Morgen-

THE PROBLEM AND THE PLAYERS

thau. Tugwell might have regarded Morgenthau as "not long on brightness," but FDR listened to his Dutchess County neighbor and friend on farm credit and monetary inflation. Berle worked feverishly on all sorts of measures, notably railroad organization. He infuriated Moley. Berle may have graduated from Harvard at the age of eighteen, but the infant prodigy, as far as Moley was concerned, had "long ceased being a prodigy and annoys me like hell by being an infant."

At the same time as Roosevelt was receiving iconoclastic ideas from the Brains Trust, he was looking to placate the old guard of the Democratic Party. He found places in his cabinet for old southern party veterans from the Wilson era, Claude Swanson of Virginia and Daniel Roper of South Carolina. He offered the Treasury to the veteran Virginia senator Carter Glass. Bernard Baruch longed to reenact his prominent role in the Wilson administration, so Roosevelt deflected him by asking him to head a team of experts preparing for the World Economic Conference. The president-elect asked the free-trade zealot Cordell Hull of Tennessee to take over the State Department.

Roosevelt's overtures to the conservatives were not merely expedient. He listened approvingly to the young Arizona congressman Lewis Douglas, appointed him director of the budget, and made it clear that economy in government would receive the highest priority. Douglas passionately believed that a balanced budget was the key to the restoration of free trade and currency stabilization. In early 1933, and in the Hundred Days, Douglas had access to FDR that was matched only by Moley's. Nor was Roosevelt dissembling when he committed himself to a balanced budget and to cutting government spending. Advisers such as Tugwell, progressives like George Norris—all believed in sound finance and were often skeptical of large-scale public works spending. Economy in government was also a popular demand. Taxpayers, particularly in rural areas, desperate to ease their tax burdens, mounted tax strikes and protests. They exercised more pressure on politicians at the state and federal level to cut government spending than did the unemployed wanting greater government largesse.

Nevertheless, Roosevelt would go only so far in assuaging the conservatives. He knew that conservative remedies would be too slow. He owed his election to the South and the West and to the farmers, and their patience would rapidly be exhausted. During the interregnum he allowed a domestic allotment bill to be taken up by Congress, and he refused to give the categorical assurances about the gold standard and sound money that Carter Glass demanded. It is clear that from January 1933 onward Roosevelt accepted the need privately for some sort of devaluation and currency inflation. The party regulars in his administration were offset by cabinet appointments of Montana progressive Tom Walsh as attorney general, Republican farm editor Henry Wallace as secretary of agriculture, Chicago reformer Harold Ickes as secretary of the interior, and New York ally Frances Perkins as secretary of labor. Whatever the uncertainty of Roosevelt's intentions about industrial recovery, the budget, and the gold standard, there could be little doubt that many of the goals of rural and regional progressivism—conservation, farm credit, water resource development, the development of public power—would be attained.

As early as January 1933, Moley foresaw that Roosevelt would be taking office under emergency conditions. From mid-February onward it was clear that Roosevelt would take office in the midst of the worst banking crisis the country had ever known. Whatever else Roosevelt planned, the absolute imperative would be to act, and to act quickly, to save the banks.

Ten Days That Opened the Banks

Closing and Reopening the Banks

As President-elect Roosevelt rode the train that took his family and closest advisers to Washington on Thursday, March 2, 1933, he talked reflectively to his future postmaster general, Jim Farley, about the economic emergency the country faced as a result of the banking crisis. Episcopalian Roosevelt told Roman Catholic Farley that the one thing that would see the people through was their firm religious faith. For Roosevelt, unlike American politicians today, religious faith was a private, understated matter. Nevertheless, on his inauguration day, Saturday, March 4, he started with a private prayer service at St. John's Episcopal Church. Later, as he sat in an anteroom at the Capitol waiting for the Senate to adjourn, he added a new opening line to his Inaugural Address, "This is a day of consecration." As he stood on the platform, he revised it: "This is a day of national consecration." After he ringingly proclaimed that "the only thing we have to fear is fear itself—nameless, unreasoning, unjustified terror which paralyzes needed efforts to convert retreat into advance," he ended his address with prayer. "In this dedication of a Nation we humbly ask the blessing of God. May He protect each and every one of us. May He guide me in the days to come." Near midnight the next day, FDR prepared to sign proclamations calling Congress into special session and declaring a national bank holiday. The Federal Reserve Board general counsel, Walter Wyatt, suggested that the effect of "the deeply religious note" on which the president ended his speech might be impaired by signing a proclamation on a Sunday. Roosevelt agreed and eventually signed the decrees at one o'clock on Monday morning.

Roosevelt's unadorned faith in divine providence bred an unshakable optimism that something would turn up. Nowhere would that faith serve him better than in his first ten days in office. That optimism enabled him to relish his new responsibilities and face with equanimity the "national economic debacle" of the closure of the nation's banks.

After the inauguration, on March 4, he returned to the White House, and Mrs. Roosevelt served hot dogs for the lunch guests. The president then reviewed the inauguration parade, giving pride of place on the stand to Mrs. Wilson and surviving members of the Wilson cabinet. While a band played the "Franklin D. Roosevelt Inauguration March," composed by the new secretary of the treasury, William Woodin, the incoming attorney general, Homer Cummings, studied the Trading with the Enemy Act of 1917. Cummings, who took office after Tom Walsh had died suddenly, decided that the Act could be used to enable the president to close the banks and halt the shipment of gold out of the country. As guests had tea at the White House, upstairs Supreme Court justice Benjamin Cardozo swore in the entire cabinet. "No cabinet has been sworn in this way before," said the president. "It is my intention to inaugurate precedents like this from time to time." He then left this "little family party" to greet a group of polio-stricken children he had invited up from Warm Springs.

These events scarcely interrupted the discussions that his advisers were having with holdover Republican officials at the Treasury and Federal Reserve Board. They wrestled with the problem of how to open the closed banks, and on Sunday they started round-the-clock discussions with leading bankers. Roosevelt went to church, briefed his cabinet, then congressional leaders, then the wire services, and finally signed the proclamations that closed the banks pending the recall of Congress. He also gave a brief radio address to the American Legion. A grudging Agnes Meyer, wife of the governor of the Federal Reserve Board, acknowledged that "We felt at once how much more quickly and easily he [FDR] arrives at decisions and one felt that many people have access to him. The country expresses relief at the thought that a positive program has begun." Hiram Johnson, the progressive Republican senator from California, was also pleasantly surprised. "The remarkable thing about him to me was his readiness to assume responsibilities and his taking those responsibilities with a smile."

On Monday, Roosevelt attended the funeral of Montana senator Thomas Walsh, his original choice for attorney general, brought state governors up to date on the banking situation, met his budget director, Lewis Douglas, to consider an economy bill, and met farm leaders. By early the next morning his advisers, Woodin and Ray Moley, had agreed on what the strategy would be for reopening the banks: they would carry out the plans outlined by the departing Republican officials for reopening and reorganizing the banks, provide adequate additional currency issued by the Federal Reserve Board, make a "tremendous gesture" for economy in government, and get the president himself to make "a man to man appeal" for public confidence.

Discussions of the banking crisis carried on all day Tuesday, and Roosevelt held his first formal cabinet meeting. By late Tuesday evening the Roosevelt advisers, the Republican officials, and congressional leaders were ready to summon Walter Wyatt to draft the banking bill. What sort of legislation do you want? he asked them. They replied, "'Ratify the Bank Holiday, preferred stock in the national banks . . . the Bank Conservation Act, and a few things like that.' I had a little slip of paper in my hand about that big, and I wrote one line on each subject. That's all I had to go by." Working without sleep, Wyatt sent his drafts back and forth to the White House. He counseled against changes: "In the few hours we've got you can't improve this thing. And you might ruin it."

On Wednesday, Roosevelt held his first, unprecedentedly relaxed and informal press conference, gave the go-ahead for introduction of farm legislation, tried to persuade Felix Frankfurter to become solicitor-general, and called to see Oliver Wendell Holmes on his ninetieth birthday. Justice Holmes drew on his Civil War experience to encourage FDR in the warlike emergency he now faced. In the evening, the president briefed congressional leaders on the banking bill.

Wyatt finally finished the bill at three on Thursday morning, March 9, and sent it to the Government Printing Office. When the House considered it in the morning a few hours later, the only copy was Wyatt's, with penciled changes. Henry Steagall, chairman of the House Banking Committee, "came down the center aisle of the House waving this thing. 'Here is this bill, let's pass it.' And they passed it." The House took forty minutes. The Senate was more deliberate, but had still passed it by 8:30 that evening.

Treasury officials now started to work frantically to see which banks could reopen. The next day Roosevelt sent his message on economy in government to Congress. On Saturday, March 11, the House voted to give the president power he had asked for to cut and reform veterans' benefits, and to cut federal salaries. Roosevelt met farm leaders and ordered the drafting of a farm bill on the basis of the agreements the leaders and Henry Wallace had reached the day before. On Sunday, Roosevelt gave his first fireside chat, describing the banking crisis in simple terms and explaining how the banks were going to reopen the following week. After his speech, he decided to ask Congress to repeal the Prohibition legislation and legalize beer. The next day, Monday, March 13, the banks reopened successfully in the twelve Federal Reserve cities.

The Blame Game

Roosevelt had matchlessly seized control of the levers of power, invoked the wartime analogy of emergency powers, and enacted an impeccably conservative program, underwriting the existing banking structure and slashing government spending.

A bitter Hoover noted that Roosevelt cheerfully carried out policies after March 4 that he had refused to endorse before, when Hoover had repeatedly implored him to cooperate to tackle the crisis. Hoover was convinced that the crisis was unnecessary and had been created by Roosevelt's refusal to cooperate. He came to believe that Roosevelt had preferred to come to power with the crisis at its worst in order to reap the maximum political credit. He took at face value comments by Rex Tugwell on February 25, reported to him from James H. Rand, Jr., that the incoming administration knew the banking structure was going to collapse and that they preferred it to be Hoover's responsibility so that they would have a "free hand" to rehabilitate the country after March 4. James P. Warburg recalled Ray Moley saying, "This is Hoover's party. We're not going to take any part in it."

For Hoover, this artificially induced "emergency" was the Trojan horse (as it had been in other revolutions) to bring in collectivist measures that would otherwise not have been sanctioned. Economic historian Robert Higgs, in *Crisis and Leviathan,* has made the identical argument. The New Dealers created an unnecessary crisis. They used the subsequent emergency to justify an unprecedented expansion of federal government powers and regulation, an expansion of state power that the American people would not have tolerated in normal times and that subsequent generations found impossible to reverse.

Raymond Moley, the Roosevelt adviser most closely involved in solving the banking crisis, rejected any notion that the crisis was artificial. On the contrary, the future of capitalism itself was under threat. That the danger of collapse was averted was due to the patriotism of the Treasury and Federal Reserve officials who had stayed on to work with Woodin, Moley, and the new administration. Putting country ahead of party, they had implemented a

sound, conservative remedy for the crisis. "If ever there was a moment when things hung in the balance, it was on March 5th,
1933—when unorthodoxy would have drained the last remaining
strength of the capitalistic system." Without "the expertness, the
information, and the plans at the lower levels of the Hoover Administration, the crisis could never have been surmounted . . .
unspeakable chaos might have followed the collapse of banking."

What Moley celebrated, progressives at the time and historians, particularly in the 1960s, lamented.

New Mexico senator Bronson Cutting looked back on the crisis "with a sick heart." It was Roosevelt's "great mistake." "The
nationalization of the banks . . . could have been accomplished
without a word of protest." Never again would a president be presented with such an opportunity. The capitalist system had ceased
to function. Congress appeared to be willing to grant the president
whatever he wanted. Roosevelt failed to capitalize on this fleeting
and unprecedented position of supreme power in the American
system and instead remained content to strengthen the existing
system.

These interpretations, both conservative and radical, overestimate the degree of calculation and foresight in Roosevelt's actions.
Roosevelt was slow to understand the extent of the crisis and did
not have revolutionary plans at hand, ready to be put into action if
emergency circumstances permitted. He had lost faith in bankers
but wanted them to be more conservative and responsible, not less.
The interpretations also overestimate the existence and availabil-
ity of radical alternatives: these alternatives were simply not presented to Roosevelt during the banking crisis, either by radical
advisers or by congressional progressives. Finally, they misunder-
stand the policy consequences of the emergency. The emergency
did not offer the chance for radical action, rather it dictated the
need for speed, which meant, in turn, the resort to existing
worked-out policies and the need for the consent of bankers and
banking officials to implement them.

The Banking Collapse

Banks in the United States failed throughout the 1920s. There were simply too many banks, too many with far too little capital. Rural small-town banks were particularly vulnerable to the strains affecting their customers: the weakness of local stores facing competition from chain stores and mail-order firms, the loss of population to the cities, expansion loans to farmers who now faced falling prices. Between 1921 and 1929, five thousand, or one quarter, of small-town banks failed. Urban banks had invested profits in securities rather than government bonds. Because corporations sought capital on the stock market rather than from bank loans, banks found themselves increasingly lending money for real estate mortgages. Between 1923 and 1929, the percentage of bank loans that were commercial fell by a fifth, while real estate loans almost tripled, and collateral loans to stock brokers increased 60 percent. Low interest rates and tax cuts in the 1920s made securities more attractive than tax-free municipal and state government bonds.

When the crash came, the collapse in farm prices made the rural banks vulnerable: their assets were now tied up in farms that could not be sold. Urban banks that had helped out these rural banks now saw them close. Falling property prices and land values made their own real estate loans risky. The falling stock market meant that they, and their customers, had to sell their securities at a loss, which drove the market down further, led more and more depositors to withdraw their savings, and left the banks with less and less cash to meet demand. Railroad bonds, once blue-chip, were now unmarketable. The European financial collapse froze more assets and led to Europeans' withdrawing gold from the United States both to protect themselves and in anticipation of an eventual American devaluation. In 1930, 1,352 banks closed, 2,294 followed in 1931, and 1,453 in 1932. Cooperative action by the bankers to pool resources in the National Credit Corporation failed. The Reconstruction Finance Corporation (RFC) was then given authority to lend money to rescue banks. Some banks collapsed nevertheless, even after receiving RFC loans; others used their loans to make their assets more liquid and increase their cash holdings and their accumulated reserves at the Federal Reserve. What they did not do, much to Hoover's intense frustration, was to make commercial loans to get the economy moving again.

From October 1932 the cumulative effects of the Depression, which had frozen so many of their assets, put strains on the strongest banks. Two hundred and ninety-seven banks failed in the last three months of 1932. The economic downturn had eroded the savings of millions of depositors. As particular banks in individual states ran into difficulties, so frightened depositors, anxious to protect whatever savings they had left, moved to withdraw their holdings from other banks as well. Successive state governors, starting in Nevada on November 1, had to call a halt to banking operations in their own states to prevent the complete collapse of every bank. In December the RFC had to intervene to save banks in Wisconsin, Pennsylvania, Minnesota, and Tennessee.

Despite the efforts of the RFC, 249 banks collapsed in January: Iowa declared a bank holiday, and Louisiana a temporary one, on February 4, to mount a rescue operation. But the final crisis was to start in Michigan, where the two leading Detroit banks had suffered from the decline both in the automobile industry and in the stock market. Henry Ford was unwilling to cooperate in an RFC rescue, and the governor of Michigan had no alternative but to call a bank holiday on February 14. Maryland, Indiana, Ohio, Arkansas, Arizona, and Oklahoma closed or restricted bank operations in the aftermath of the Michigan collapse. Money bled out of the banks altogether or moved from the weaker banks to the stronger banks. Europeans started to withdraw gold in record quantities. Sixteen states called bank holidays on March 1 and 2, another nine limited withdrawals. Finally, on the morning of March 4, Illinois and New York shut their banks.

Hoover and the Policy Options

In reacting to the quickening bank crisis, Treasury and Federal Reserve Board officials had already developed detailed plans that included three of the crucial aspects of what would be the Roosevelt banking rescue package: a national banking holiday, authority to open closed banks, and the purchase of preferred stock in banks by the RFC.

On three occasions in 1932, the Hoover administration had considered a national banking holiday. Walter Wyatt noted that back in 1918 he had made amendments to the Trading with the Enemy Act precisely for such an eventuality. In mid-February 1933, George Harrison of the New York Federal Reserve Board and Wyatt, backed by Treasury secretary Mills, urged Hoover to declare a national bank holiday under the Trading with the Enemy Act, to give them breathing space to reorganize the banks. In the desperate straits of March 2 and 3, even the Federal Reserve Board agreed it could support a national bank holiday, and Wyatt drafted a proclamation closing the banks based on the 1917 act.

But how could banks be reopened once they had been closed? Acting comptroller of the currency F. Gloyd Awalt had recognized this difficulty of quickly reorganizing and reopening closed banks. If a receiver were appointed, that would almost guarantee lengthy or permanent closure if a few depositors or stockholders proved uncooperative and demanded immediate first claim on existing assets. In February, Awalt and Wyatt drafted a bank conservation bill that would allow the appointment of a conservator who could restructure the bank and force depositors to forgo immediate repayment.

The RFC had made loans of more than $2 billion and still had not saved either the banks or the economy. What the banks needed was not greater indebtedness but a long-term injection of working capital. In the summer of 1932, the idea of the RFC investing in preferred stock was broached. In December, Eugene Meyer at the

Federal Reserve Board advocated it. In January 1933, Hoover told Wyatt and Awalt to draft a bill. Awalt kept a copy of the bill in his safe.

If the broad outlines of the New Deal response to the crisis had already been mapped out by Hoover's officials, why did Hoover not act on these proposals?

In part, Hoover's response was ideological. He had never really approved of the RFC—the idea of a permanent RFC not just making loans but controlling bank capital smacked too much of government ownership and collectivism. Bank conservators, for their part, would infringe on private property rights. Only at the end did he accept that any bank holiday would have to be associated with some sort of reorganization. In both cases, Hoover could rightly point out that the Democrats in Congress were unlikely to pass such legislation.

More had to do with Hoover's reluctance to admit that his policies had failed, his unwillingness to help those who he felt had betrayed him, and a persistent effort to blame others for his troubles.

Eugene Meyer, chairman of the Federal Reserve, recalled the last month of Hoover's government as "a period of going along as best you could from day to day, knowing that you weren't getting anything except black looks in the White House. . . . He [Hoover] went into a tailspin mentally—emotionally. He'd taken an awful licking in the election. He had all these problems and was trying to get Roosevelt to cooperate in his own way—the Hoover way. He was very suspicious that people in his crowd were playing with Roosevelt, which a lot of them did."

Meyer's wife was less charitable. Hoover, she wrote in her diary on February 25, is busy "making a record—writing messages to Congress, letters to Fed. Res. Bd. offering new laws (which he couldn't get passed) etc. . . . national and international disaster never helped him to rid himself of his highly emotional, immature, egotistical fixations. . . . Looking back it seems like nothing but blunder after blunder."

It grieved Hoover to have to act to rescue bankers who, he believed, were responsible for their own plight or to plead with the Federal Reserve Board, which had, as far as he was concerned, acted with "criminal passivity." On March 2 he told Agnes Meyer, "Eugene and I have tried everything on behalf of the bankers but they have fought us, haven't tried to cooperate . . . haven't even told the truth. They are without ability and without character . . . It would have been better if Gene and I had never tried to save the banks. If we had let them go, we'd be all over it now." On March 3, when Eugene Meyer pleaded with him to proclaim a bank holiday, Hoover saw no need to act precipitately to aid the bankers, whose selfishness had so often thwarted his appeals for voluntary cooperative action. "I can keep on fiddling," he grimly remarked, "they have been fiddling long enough and I can do some fiddling myself."

At first, he resisted a bank holiday because he believed other actions might work and render one unnecessary: more RFC loans, guaranteed deposits, clearinghouse certificates as currency, aggressive Federal Reserve open-market operations. These were either politically impossible or likely to have only a marginal impact. At the end he would not proclaim a holiday unless Roosevelt endorsed it, appealing to him at a social tea at the White House on March 3 and ringing him at eleven that night, and again at 1:30 a.m.

Hoover firmly believed that the reason for the loss of confidence was that depositors were afraid of the radicalism of the incoming Roosevelt administration. He had attempted to convey the gravity of the situation to FDR in a ten-page handwritten appeal delivered by a Secret Service agent late on Saturday night, February 18. Hoover said the panic could be halted if Roosevelt issued a statement committing himself to balance the budget even at the cost of extra taxation, to maintain government credit, and to rule out any currency inflation. As Hoover admitted two days later to Senator David Reed, such a commitment would require the abandonment of 90 percent of the New Deal.

In Hoover's own State Department, the economic adviser Herbert Feis was unimpressed:

> When a copy of this letter was shown to me, I sniffed. Its ideas and words were echoes of those of Mills [Treasury secretary] and the big bankers. None of them could face the fact that their own policies during the previous decade had fostered the depression. They were taking refuge in the belief that the soundness of the policies and actions would be proven if only the President-Elect and the inflationist members of Congress and other groups would stop scaring the American people.

Why did Roosevelt refuse to acknowledge the February 18 letter and why did he later refuse to cooperate in instituting a bank holiday, especially as he intended to close the banks anyway?

It was understandable that he declined voluntarily to forgo his domestic New Deal as Hoover asked on February 18. Though Roosevelt fully intended to balance the budget, it was also clear that he was not certain that the United States could stay on the gold standard: some form of devaluation and currency inflation had clearly not been ruled out by Roosevelt and many of his advisers.

Roosevelt also may not have appreciated the gravity of the situation. He rather glibly said that the trouble with the banks was that many did not have sufficient assets to meet demands, a statement that implied that there was little anybody could do about it. He had little sympathy for the bankers, whose malpractice was being exposed by Ferdinand Pecora's investigation for the Senate Banking and Currency Committee. He would excoriate their selfishness in his inaugural. His blithe optimism may have blinded him to the harsh realities. Certainly he appears to have done little to make plans for a bank holiday, except for his own inquiries into the validity of the Trading with the Enemy Act and the collection of the proclamations of various state governors closing their banks. As Walter Wyatt recalled, neither Roosevelt nor his advisers had any plans for dealing with the banking crisis. "I was absolutely amazed. There wasn't anybody in that entire Brains Trust, apparently, that had given any thought—they certainly had no plans—or any real study to the problem created by this banking situation."

There was a desperate irony in these last-ditch appeals of Hoover to the incoming president to join him in instituting the bank holiday late on March 3. He had been arguing right to the end that it was the businessmen's fear of Roosevelt that inhibited the business confidence necessary to stem the economic collapse. Now he argued that only Roosevelt could instill that confidence. It is perhaps not surprising that Roosevelt chose not to dissipate his prestige by joining a discredited president in what might have been a futile effort to maintain business and depositor confidence.

What is clear is that Roosevelt did not intend to use the crisis to secure vast new government powers in the emergency. When he issued the call on March 4 to Congress to come into special session to deal with the banking crisis, he had no elaborate plans to seek increased government powers over the economy. He was soon persuaded to take advantage of Congress's presence to ask for farm legislation and assistance to the unemployed, but that was all. But he did unhesitatingly exploit the warlike emergency for one grant of unprecedented presidential authority. He did seek, and won, in the Economy Act, executive powers to slash government spending, which would never have been granted in normal circumstances. The emergency was initially therefore to be used to *reduce*, not expand, the functions of government.

Roosevelt Takes Charge

Once the banks had closed in the early hours of March 4, the overwhelming priority had to be to reopen them as quickly as possible. The country could survive for a few days without normal banking facilities: ingenuity could and did meet individual cash demands; some leeway was given to banks to meet some essential services and existing payrolls. But soon the economy would grind to a complete halt. A prolonged bank closure would worsen the existing depression: all too many assets were tied up already in closed banks, bankrupt companies, foreclosed homes and farms. An extended bank holiday would have completed the devastation.

The Roosevelt administration simply did not have any idea about how to reopen the banks. It had no alternative but to turn to the departing Republican officials. The measures to tackle the banking crisis and to reopen the banks drew directly on the plans already in place, those drafted by Treasury and Federal Reserve officials.

The new attorney general, New Hampshire Democratic stalwart Homer Cummings, was prepared to give a clear ruling, unlike his predecessor, that the president had the authority to use his powers under the Trading with the Enemy Act to proclaim a national three-day bank holiday. Such a holiday would give Congress time to assemble. Walter Wyatt showed Cummings the proclamation he had already drafted, closing the banks and halting the export of gold, and the attorney general approved it—and FDR signed it early on March 6.

When William Woodin and Ray Moley left Roosevelt's hotel room in the early hours of Saturday morning, the day of the inauguration, they saw the lights on in the Treasury building and went over to find Secretary Ogden Mills and Undersecretary Arthur Ballantine still frantically trying to seek last-minute solutions. The new team freely confessed their ignorance, and Mills and Ballantine agreed to stay on to help them. There was no love lost between the blustering, arrogant Mills and his fellow New Yorker Roosevelt, but Mills had both the mastery of the details of the banking situation and the technicians on hand that the new government needed. Through Saturday, Mills and his officials worked on a rescue package, which they presented to the conference of bankers, Federal Reserve officials, congressional representatives, and Woodin and Moley on Sunday morning. The key was the recognition that maybe a third of the banks could reopen straightaway. Another group of banks could never reopen. The problem was how to reopen the third group of the more problematic banks. Here Mills could turn to the bill Awalt had drafted for bank conservators: these conservators could reorganize such banks and not have to worry that creditors would thwart these plans by demanding first claim on the banks' assets. But more was needed to strengthen these banks. The bankers themselves wanted the federal guarantee of deposits. Roosevelt, his views conveyed by Woodin, adamantly refused to bail out irresponsible bankers that way. The alternative was the measure Wyatt had drafted to allow the Reconstruction Finance Corporation to buy preferred stock in these banks and increase their capital. This bill was brought out of Awalt's safe and put into the package.

What troubled the conferees throughout Sunday and Monday was what would happen when the banks reopened and needed actual currency to pay out to customers. There were not enough bank notes in circulation, backed by gold, to use. For a long time it looked as if there would have to be some form of scrip, a special currency issued by the clearinghouse banks, which everybody feared would drive "real" currency out of circulation and fuel massive, uncontrolled inflation. Roosevelt's own proposal for redeeming outstanding government bonds with paper money seemed even worse. Another holdover official, Federal Reserve staffer Eugene Goldenweiser, had the answer: currency issued by the Federal Reserve against the assets of sound banks, money that looked like money.

By Tuesday morning the outlines of the banking rescue package were clearly laid out. The scheme could work only if depositors had confidence when the banks reopened—otherwise the runs on the reopened banks, however sound they might be, would continue unabated. Two devices were considered essential to that confidence. A major gesture toward economy—Roosevelt's plans to slash government spending, worked out with budget director Lewis Douglas on Monday—and a personal appeal to the nation by the president himself.

The Banking Act that Wyatt drafted incorporating the results of the negotiations owed most to the technicians, the holdover experts from the Treasury and the Federal Reserve, Awalt, Wyatt, and Goldenweiser. Mills and Ballantine put this material together. Woodin and Moley had to weigh it up—Moley was probably the only member of Roosevelt's close circle who understood all the details. The people who did not have much input into the banking policy were the bankers and the president. As Woodin told the president on March 5, the bankers' representatives were "very much at sea as to what to do." Roosevelt himself largely delegated to Woodin and Moley the conduct of negotiations and relied on their judgment as to the soundness of the policy proposals. His own proposal for money to redeem bonds was rejected. His rejection of government insurance of bank deposits was, however, decisive for the time being.

A more radical policy, nationalizing the banks, was never discussed. This alternative was simply not available if the banks were to be reopened quickly. On Wednesday, March 8, progressive senators Robert La Follette, Jr., of Wisconsin, and Edward P. Costigan, of Colorado, went to see Roosevelt with a memorandum proposing more federal control of a unified banking system. But after talking to FDR, they did not leave the memorandum with him, and it was certainly not a proposal for nationalizing the banks as fellow progressive Bronson Cutting later liked to remember. Indeed, Cutting, who was not even in Washington in March 1933, actually thought during the banking crisis itself that Roosevelt "had handled the problem well." Even if taking the banks into public ownership had been a policy option raised during the crisis, it could not have been put into action quickly enough to solve the immediate problem of helping millions of depositors. The United States simply did not have the "state capacity" in 1933 to effect such a radical solution. Both the lament that a radical opportunity was missed and Moley's self-congratulation that capitalism was saved and radicalism averted fail to recognize that there was no practical radical alternative, or pressure for it, available in the emergency of March 1933.

Roosevelt and Confidence: The Press

Roosevelt liked to make a firm distinction between newspaper owners, whom he regarded as his opponents, and journalists, whom he considered his friends. In fact, in response to the refreshing confidence of the inaugural, newspaper proprietors and their editors enthusiastically backed the new president. Captain Joseph Patterson, owner of the New York *Daily News*, pledged to support "whatever Mr. Roosevelt may urge as methods of attacking these emergencies." Roy Howard assured FDR's press secretary, Steve Early, that his editors had been directed to praise the president. Even the *Chicago Tribune* editor and publisher Colonel Robert McCormick praised the embargo on gold shipments and the bank holiday. Columnist Walter Lippmann, writing to a doubtful Felix Frankfurter on March 8, was in no doubt that the time for discussion and reflection was over: "the character of this crisis requires extraordinary measures."

That same day, Roosevelt held his first press conference. Hoover's relations with the press had, Paul Anderson said back in 1931, "reached a state of unpleasantness without parallel during the present century." By contrast, from January 1 to the inauguration, Roosevelt had seen the press daily. At 10:10 on March 8, a hundred press men crowded into the Oval Office for Roosevelt's first presidential press conference, and Roosevelt shook each one of them by the hand. As he told the newsmen, he had been told "that what I am about to do will become impossible" but he was going to try it. He established ground rules for the conferences—the abolition of written questions; direct quotation only in writing from his press secretary, Steve Early; news announcements without quotation; background material not for attribution; and off-the-record comments were to remain confidential; he would not answer "iffy" questions; press conferences would alternate between 10:00 and 4:30, to give equal opportunity to the morning and evening papers. That first conference set the pattern. FDR bantered easily with correspondents (all male and all white), whom he called by their first names. He displayed a mastery of detail that would continue to astound journalists. He made life easier for them by explaining the complex banking situation in terms that they could understand and convey to their readers. Above all, he provided them with news. As one correspondent estimated, "in that first sitting . . . the new president gave the correspondents more sensational news than some of his predecessors had handed out in four years." It was the first of 377 press conferences in Roosevelt's first term. The hard-boiled newsmen were bowled over and spontaneously applauded. The studied casualness of FDR was not effortless, as Jimmy Byrnes noted at an early press conference: "his hand was trembling and he was wet with perspiration."

Roosevelt and Confidence: Congress and the Radio

When Henry Steagall brought the banking bill to the House of Representatives the next day, congressmen were not disposed to debate the finer points. As the Republican minority leader Bertrand Snell explained,

> Of course, it is entirely out of the ordinary to pass legislation in this house that, as far as I know, is not even in print at the time it is offered. . . . The house is burning down and

the president of the United States says this is the way to put out the fire. And to me at this time, there is only one answer to that question and that is to give the president what he demands and says is necessary to meet the situation.

The bill passed with a voice vote. In the Senate, the veteran Virginia senator Carter Glass, possibly the only member of the Congress who understood the technicalities of the legislation, guided the bill through. There was some unease on the part of southern and western progressives. The flamboyant Huey Long from Louisiana worried about the impact on depositors and small state banks. "All sorts of wild charges," claimed the bill's drafter, Walter Wyatt. "Finally Senator Glass showed [Long] up by saying that he didn't know what he was talking about." Glass, who was suspicious of Roosevelt's intentions over currency inflation, nevertheless considered himself the personal embodiment and fount of all wisdom on the Federal Reserve system and trusted Wyatt and the other Federal Reserve professionals. In the end only a handful of progressive Republican senators voted against the legislation. The bill passed both houses within ten hours of being introduced. The economy bill that Roosevelt secured two days later aroused much more substantial opposition: conservative Republican support was vital for its passage.

Once the bill passed, Treasury and Federal Reserve officials had to work round the clock to find out what banks could be safely reopened. If they reopened too many, they risked a liquidity crisis. If they reopened too few, they risked further deflation. The speed with which they had to act left officials in Washington no alternative but to rely on state banking authorities—and the bankers on them—who were the only ones likely to have the necessary information about the condition of local banks. They opted for a relatively liberal policy, erring on the side of opening too many banks. There was not enough time to open banks on Friday, as Roosevelt had believed, but they hoped for a phased reopening on the first three days of the following week.

These decisions, based on inadequate data, were a gamble. Would Americans have the confidence to leave their money in, and even return their money to, the reopened banks?

From the start Roosevelt's advisers believed that the key to persuading the American public to deposit, not withdraw, their cash, would be what they envisaged as a "man to man appeal for public confidence" from the president. Roosevelt went on the radio on Sunday evening, March 12, to deliver the first of what Harry Butcher, manager of the CBS Washington bureau, would subsequently christen "fireside chats." Roosevelt liked "to think of his audience as being a few people round his fireplace," but he prepared with meticulous care everything from the correct angle of the microphone, to a false tooth to close a gap in his first two lower teeth, to the speed of his delivery—about one hundred words a minute—to the language he used; more than three quarters of the words were among the thousand most commonly used words. He explained the phased reopening of the banks, assured his listeners that no sound bank "is a dollar worse off than it was when it closed its doors last week," promised them that there was enough money—"sound currency because it is backed by actual assets"— and reiterated that "there is nothing complex, nothing radical in the process." The heart of the appeal was his "assurance, my friends, that it is safer to keep your money in a reopened bank than it is to keep it under the mattress."

Roosevelt had identified confidence as the key. "Confidence and courage are the essentials of success in carrying out our plan. You people must have faith; you must not be stampeded by rumors or guesses." Walter Wyatt listened in admiration. Roosevelt, he thought, "showed more understanding about [the fireside chat] than any member of his Brains Trust I knew." Agnes Meyer observed with wonder the response to Roosevelt's appeal on the first day, when the banks in the twelve Federal Reserve cities opened. "The banks opened today in the big cities in an unexpected calm. People are behaving wonderfully. The sale of Gov. Bonds will be completed long before three o'clock. Two N Y banks each took $1,000,000." She acerbically noted the next day, "Everybody is amazed at the faith with which the populace accepts the re-opening of the banks. No-body is more surprised than the bankers themselves." In three days, 70 percent of the banks, more than 12,000, reopened. In the next month another 1,300 reopened. When the dust had settled, 3,100 banks were reorganized, with the RFC buying preferred stock in the banks, and only 1,100 were liquidated. In the rest of the year, only 221 banks failed. The measure of the high stakes Roosevelt was playing for, and the extent of his accomplishment, should not be underestimated. Just a year earlier Hoover had made a similar national appeal to bank depositors not to hoard their cash. His appeal failed as spectacularly as Roosevelt's suc-ceeded.

At his March 8 press conference, Roosevelt had said, "We can-not write a permanent banking act for the nation in three days." He also expressed himself as firmly opposed to the federal guaran-tee of bank deposits: "you guarantee bad banks as well as good banks and the minute the government starts to do that the govern-ment runs into a probable loss." By the end of the Hundred Days, Roosevelt would have his permanent banking legislation, the Glass-Steagall Act, signed into law on June 16. Advocates of strong national banks and branch banking as a way of solving the problem of too many small, undercapitalized banks failed to se-cure any dramatic change in banking structures, though restric-tions on branch banking were eased a little. The revelations of financial chicanery in the Pecora hearings made the proposal to separate commercial and investment banking unstoppable. In an effort to improve the record of the Federal Reserve in monetary management, control of open-market interventions was moved from New York to Washington, under the control of the Federal Reserve Board.

But Roosevelt continued to resist the guarantee of bank de-posits. Such a proposal had been introduced in Congress many

times and had failed: some state deposit insurance schemes had
been enacted, but they either were repealed or lay dormant. Roosevelt, like the large bankers, feared that strong banks would be
pulled under by bailing out weaker ones. He threatened to veto the
banking act. But in the end, midwestern politicians such as Arthur
Vandenberg, and southern and western leaders such as Vice President Garner, Banking Committee chairman Henry Steagall, and
California senator William Gibbs McAdoo, tapped into too powerful a constituency sentiment: suspicious of the power of eastern
bankers, they warned that depositors would simply not keep their
money in the banks unless there was some form of deposit guarantee. Roosevelt capitulated, and the Federal Deposit Insurance
Corporation was one of the great success stories of the New
Deal. The mere existence of deposit guarantees ensured that they
would not be needed. Between 1921 and 1933 Americans had lost
$146 million a year in closed banks. Between 1934 and 1960 they
lost on average $706,000 a year. Together with greater control of
the Federal Reserve in 1935, the banking acts of 1933 heralded
unprecedented stability in the American banking system. The
bankers who benefited had had almost nothing to do with the
measures that rescued them.

Quick Action: The Conservative Restraint

Hiram Johnson, who had watched Roosevelt at close quarters in
the conferences on Sunday and Wednesday evening, marveled at
the end of the week not only at what the president had accomplished but at his seemingly unflappable temperament.

> I do not see how any living soul can last physically going the
> pace that he is going, and mentally any one of us would be
> a psychopathic case if we undertook to do what he is doing.
> And with it all, the amazing thing to me was there never

was a note of impatience in all the hours we sat there Wednesday night, or the previous Sunday, and never anything but the utmost good nature.

But the work was only just beginning. Opening the banks quickly had been the inevitable first, and unexpected, goal of the new administration. Lacking radical plans, worked-out alternatives, or the "state capacity" to implement rapid reform, Roosevelt had had to turn to the ready-made plans and expertise of Treasury and Federal Reserve officials who had been denied the opportunity by the suspicious and beleaguered Hoover to put their plans into practice. Ten days to reopen the banks dictated that the existing banking system would be only shored up rather than radically transformed.

Reopening the banks was a necessary prerequisite for economic recovery and for the New Deal. But in itself, it contributed little to stimulate renewed economic growth. Even the injection of additional capital from the RFC into the banks tended to liquefy banks' assets rather than dramatically increase commercial credit. Would Roosevelt be as conservative in his recovery and relief programs as he had been in the rescue of the banks?

THREE

First Priorities

On March 12, 1933, the budget director, Lewis Douglas, wrote to his father:

> It seems queer to telephone at any hour to a president, to go into his bedroom at one in the morning, in fact to have the entre [*sic*] at any time and to be writing a presidential message to Congress on the budget. How strange for an insignificant man from Arizona to be in such a position. When I stop to think about it all it is quite frightening.

The secretary of labor, Frances Perkins, told one of her assistants that "every proposition presented at Cabinet meetings is referred to him [Douglas] to see how it affects the Budget and once it is referred his suggestions are not generally limited to finance." Douglas's visibility at the start of the Hundred Days is powerful testimony to the importance Roosevelt placed on controlling government spending. Part of the rescue package for the banks that Ray Moley and Secretary Woodin placed before Roosevelt on Tuesday, March 7, had called for a "tremendous gesture" in economy in government. Roosevelt determined that he would not lose the momentum gained by the rapid passage of banking legislation. He decided to keep Congress in session to take action in his areas of highest priority. After all, the banking measures in themselves put no one back to work, and saved not a single farm or home. On

March 8, Roosevelt indicated that he wanted Congress to stay in session. By the end of the week it was clear that he would demand measures to cut government spending, the establishment of a "tree army" to put the urban unemployed to work in the countryside on conservation measures, and the enactment of farm-recovery legislation.

Slashing Government Spending

"The economy phase of the New Deal," noted the historian Frank Freidel, "was not an aberration but one aspect of the overall program in which Roosevelt never lost faith." Between 1789 and 1932 only one third of the federal government's annual budgets were unbalanced. Balanced budgets had been the norm in the 1920s. But federal government spending was limited then. Federal spending of $2.9 billion, for example in the fiscal year ending June 1929, represented only 2.8 percent of GNP. The limited functions of the federal government were funded largely by indirect taxation, notably the tariff. Few Americans paid the federal income tax that had finally been approved by the Sixteenth Amendment to the Constitution in 1913. Recessions always threatened a balanced budget, and Hoover was unworried by the deficits in fiscal years 1930 and 1931, but the deficit for fiscal year 1932 reached 4.6 percent of GNP. To Hoover and his Treasury secretary, Ogden Mills, government borrowing to fund that deficit was restricting the credit that banks could make available to businesses. Government spending, and wild, Depression-induced proposals to increase that spending, threatened business confidence. A balanced budget became a key target for the Hoover program as part of the package that would bring the international revival that was the precondition of American recovery—currency stabilization, fiscal restraint, and the removal of world trade barriers. Hoover attempted to raise government revenue by introducing a federal sales tax. Despite his failure to secure that tax, the Revenue Act of 1932 represented the largest peacetime tax increase in American history.

A balanced budget was not merely the shibboleth of conservative businessmen. Most political leaders, on the left and the right, believed in fiscal orthodoxy. Roosevelt understood that the business and investment communities wanted sound finance. In a campaign speech in Pittsburgh, Roosevelt memorably assailed the waste and extravagance of the Hoover administration and promised to slash government spending by 25 percent. Labor leader William Green and Chamber of Commerce president Henry Harriman called on Roosevelt to cut spending in order to expand credit, stimulate investment, and encourage entrepreneurs. Historians, argues David Beito, have ignored "the significant *popular* base beneath economy-in-government sentiment." In the 1920s, taxes had doubled as a percentage of national income, but between 1929 and 1932 they rose from 11.6 percent to 21.1 percent. The tax burden fell disproportionately on homeowners who, already struggling to meet mortgage repayments, now struggled to pay property taxes. By January 1933 one local government expert reported, "Demands for indiscriminate budget slashing are the order of the day. So-called economy leagues are springing up all over the country. Embattled taxpayers are organizing strikes. Fluent orators are taking to the air to attack government and the cost of government." Taxpayers' leagues could be numbered in their thousands by 1932, and in the spring of 1933, as Roosevelt took office, several hundred more were formed.

But if politicians heard from angry taxpayers critically examining how government spent their tax dollars, they also heard desperate constituent demands for increased spending and government assistance. No group was more vociferous than veterans of World War I. The well-organized veterans' lobby had secured ever more favorable treatment from Congress since 1918. Veterans received benefits to compensate for injuries sustained in the war, and Congress had steadily increased the range of disabilities that veterans could claim assistance for, even though those illnesses might not be service-related. By fiscal year 1933, spending on veterans accounted for close to $1 billion, almost a quarter of the federal budget, paid to a mere 1 percent of the population. But veterans demanded even greater assistance during the Depression.

At the end of the war, Congress had given returning soldiers a sixty-dollar severance bonus. This sum looked ungenerous in the light of wartime price inflation and the high wages that workers at home had received. In 1924 Congress had attempted to address that grievance by providing for an adjusted service-compensation payment to veterans in 1945. As the Depression hit, many veterans demanded immediate payment of that compensation—which became known as the veterans' bonus. To veterans, this payment was not a bonus, but the repayment of a debt the United States owed them. To politicians like the young East Texas congressman Wright Patman, the bonus would not only provide assistance to struggling veterans but would also redirect currency to depressed rural areas and provide much-needed currency inflation. To business leaders; officials of the veterans' own organization, the American Legion; Democratic congressional leaders; and Hoover's White House, the bonus was a special-interest "gimme" demand, a reckless and irresponsible raid on the Federal Treasury. Hoover had threatened to veto any bonus legislation and had watched troops brutally remove the veterans who had camped in Washington in the summer of 1932. On March 9, 1933, Wright Patman reintroduced a bill to provide for currency expansion and the bonus. Every congressman had veterans in his district; their pressure was a powerful counterweight to any move to cut government spending.

No one was more aware of the power of the veterans' lobby than Lewis Douglas. As Arizona's lone congressman, he had called in May 1932 for a 20 percent reduction in veterans' benefits. Ex-servicemen represented 20 percent of his electorate, and he was defeated. Douglas's grandfather, a mining consultant, had created a fortune in pioneer-era Arizona based on copper. His father, "Rawhide Jimmy," was a harsh frontiersman yet also a friend of the French wartime leader Georges Clemenceau, whose home he paid for. Lewis Douglas combined chivalrous manners, a keen intellect, and a love of frontier life. Decorated in World War I, he was a teaching assistant at Amherst in 1920 to visiting British professors Ernest Barker and R. H. Tawney. Elected to succeed Carl Hayden as Arizona's congressman, he found himself with friends on both sides of the political aisle. A consistent opponent of pork barrel legislation, even when it benefited Arizona, he regarded House speaker John Nance Garner, of Texas, with particular contempt: "a cheap yellow trickster with neither intelligence, mental honesty or courage—a man completely and absolutely unqualified to hold a position of high public responsibility." Douglas was convinced that politicians such as Garner had to be disciplined. A balanced budget would exert that discipline. In 1932, Douglas introduced a resolution establishing an economy committee in Congress and was appointed to it. His remedy for the Depression was absolutely clear: "First, actually balance the budget, second face the question of reviving world trade, which, of course, means debts, stabilizing exchange and liberalizing tariffs." The last part of this internationalist option reflected both Douglas's belief that the Smoot-Hawley Tariff was the main cause of the Depression and his friendship with Cordell Hull, his "father confessor and guide."

When Douglas met Roosevelt, he was pleased by the president-elect's emphasis on government economy and tariff reduction. Although he wanted FDR to cooperate with Hoover over debts, he allowed himself to be persuaded by Roosevelt's argument that he did not want to join in an open cooperative effort with a repudiated president. He believed Roosevelt would take steps to secure a debt settlement. Brains Trusters, for their part, were charmed by Douglas, who, according to Tugwell, was "very intelligent." Tugwell "liked him a lot, wondered at it in a congressman." Douglas made it clear to Roosevelt that the "future of civilization itself" depended on an actual balanced budget. Persuaded that FDR was absolutely committed to that goal, Douglas accepted the position of budget director.

During the hectic bank negotiations on March 6 and 7, Roosevelt and Douglas looked at a draft economy bill. Economy in government was one of the few areas where detailed policy proposals had already been worked out. During the interregnum, the congressional committee that Douglas had initiated had drawn up proposals that would cut almost $1 billion from a $4 billion budget for fiscal year 1934. By March 8, Douglas had a bill ready, which Roosevelt transmitted to Congress with a strong message of presidential support on March 10. "Too often," said Roosevelt, "in recent history liberal governments have been wrecked on the rocks of loose fiscal policy." The bill delegated to the president broad executive powers to overhaul and slim down the veterans' benefit system and to cut federal salaries by up to 15 percent.

It was a measure of Roosevelt's immense prestige in that first week of the New Deal that the House of Representatives passed the Economy Bill the next day. It was a bitter pill for Congress to swallow. No matter how unpopular government jobholders were with taxpayers, jobs were the lifeblood of the patronage system on which a congressman's future depended. They knew they would hear from the powerful veterans' lobby. Nevertheless, a quick vote forestalled the mobilization of the veterans' lobby, and the broad grant of executive power shifted the responsibility and opprobrium for specific cuts from Congress to the president. Even so, seventy-two Republican House votes were critical to passage of the bill, countering the defection of ninety Democrats. Douglas's friend Virginia congressman Clifford Woodrum, who was a zealous member of the House Appropriations Committee, warned his fellow Democrats that Roosevelt would look at the roll call to see who was "willing to go along with him in this great fight to save the country." This threat was real. The stance of a congressman on the Economy Bill was the single most important factor in decisions in the Hundred Days on whom to reward or not to reward with patronage.

To soften the blow, Roosevelt recommended on Monday the legalization of beer. The lame-duck Congress had repealed the Prohibition amendment, but it awaited ratification by the states. Legalizing the sale of 3.2 percent beer was possible in advance of repeal. Such a move was popular with urban congressmen, but it also appealed to the advocates of economy in government. Lewis Douglas had advocated it the previous summer in order to raise $100 million in excise taxes, which could have helped balance the budget. Conservative businessmen who supported the Association Against the Prohibition Amendment rejoiced. Within a week of legal beer being available in nineteen states, an estimated $4 million was paid in additional taxes. Legalization of beer passed Congress almost at once. In this almost casual and tangential way, Roosevelt eliminated the ethnocultural issue that had plagued national politics for twenty years. At the same time, the president's message eased the passage of the Economy Act in the Senate on March 15, after two days of debate in which conservative Republican votes again came to the rescue of the president to defeat liberal Democratic amendments.

Douglas was delighted. The president, he told his father, "has been magnificent. He flirts with ideas, has imagination, is rather slow to come to definitive decisions, but when he finally does is willing to go through to the end." Douglas met with the president every day: they abolished agencies here, consolidated others there. He revamped the veterans' benefits program in order to cut that expenditure by over 30 percent in 1934. In the next twelve months, Douglas was able to cut government spending by reducing the defense budget by $125 million, Post Office costs by $75 million, and government salaries by $75 million, and saved $100 million through staff reorganization. Douglas believed that these economies would not only stimulate economic recovery but also enable the government to fulfill its humanitarian aims. When another Bonus Army of unemployed veterans arrived in Washington, Roosevelt dispersed them not with troops but with a visit from Eleanor Roosevelt. He offered them loans on the security of their future bonus and jobs in the newly created Civilian Conservation Corps.

Douglas fought a consistent and powerful battle to restrain government spending during the rest of the Hundred Days. Advisers such as Rex Tugwell thought him all too powerful because he was so easy to like. But Douglas's vigilance would come up against strong countervailing forces: humanitarian demands for spending, the pressure to increase domestic prices, and the impossibility of raising government revenue through increased income taxes. Douglas would wring his hands at the idea of a "double" budget (a non-emergency one that would be balanced, and an emergency deficit that would be exceptional). He was horrified by the departure from the gold standard and by the collapse at the London conference of the internationalist option of debt settlement, currency stabilization, and tariff reduction. But it is important to remember that, at the end of the Hundred Days, Douglas was still a major figure in the administration. He acknowledged to Walter Lippmann on June 27 that he had not won "entirely, as far as discipline is concerned." The odds may be against them, and several defeats may come back to haunt them, but it was "a struggle in which it is well worth while to be a participant."

A Tree Army

On March 8, Roosevelt found time in the midst of the banking crisis to write to Nelson Brown at the New York State College of Forestry, at Syracuse, about the trees planted in each of the past two years on the experimental acreage on his Creek Road Farm at Hyde Park. He had cleared another five acres for the college to plant. He also wanted Brown to "make a note to having a careful

inspection made of the swamp area planted last year. The permanent tree crop consisted of tulip poplars and black walnuts and
these were interspaced with, I think, red cedar and larch. The
planting should be filled out to replace trees that have died. During the winter I had all the sprouts cut off from the stumps of the
old trees that had been cut."

There could be no doubting Roosevelt's passionate concern for
forest conservation. As governor of New York he had sought funds
in 1929 to put jobless men to work on forestry schemes, and by
1932 ten thousand were employed. In his acceptance speech at the
Democratic National Convention he talked of a million men to be
put to work to fight soil erosion and replenish cutover land. On the
afternoon of March 9 he summoned the secretaries of agriculture,
the interior, and war to outline his plans to take possibly half a million young men out of the cities and put them in camps where
they would plant trees, protect forests, and control floods. Told to
bring a bill back by 9:30 p.m., Interior solicitor Edward Finney
and Judge Advocate General Kyle Rucker took the draft up to
Roosevelt's study at nine o'clock. Roosevelt noted that Finney had
failed to provide for condemnation of private property. Finney
dictated a suitable section and removed, at Louis Howe's suggestion, the military term "enlistment."

Douglas was happy to approve the proposal because it did not
need additional funding at that point, and it served to dampen demands for more wide-ranging public works programs. Advocates
of those programs feared a preemptive strike and persuaded Roosevelt to ask Harold Ickes to be a clearinghouse for such plans, but
Roosevelt also asked Ickes, Secretary of War George Dern, and
Henry Wallace to go ahead with plans for the Civilian Conservation Corps. Roosevelt told the press on March 15, and Congress
on March 21, that he would consider wider relief proposals in due
course. For the time being, he was concerned about the forests and
the spiritual benefits that could come from taking city boys to the
forestry camps. If care were not taken thinning existing forests,

the United States would, within thirty to forty years, exhaust its natural lumber resources and would become a very large lumber-importing nation. Vast damage done by floods in Ohio also highlighted the urgency. Roosevelt promised Congress that people could be put to work within two weeks of passage of the act. He foresaw not only material benefits but "the moral and spiritual value of such work . . . We can take a vast army of these unemployed out into healthful surroundings. We can eliminate to some extent at least the threat that enforced idleness brings to spiritual and moral stability." Congress responded by passing the bill within a week, and Roosevelt signed it on March 31.

Roosevelt needed to move quickly to fulfill his promises. Only the army and army facilities could process the applicants, assemble them, and transport them to distant camps. FDR, like Louis Howe, was nervous about charges of militarism, especially as Hitler's work camps also aimed to employ young men who were "rotting helplessly in the streets." He asked a reporter not to call the enlistment centers "concentration camps" or even "cantonments." He hoped the enrollees would be there only a week. Although the camps themselves would be run by the military, the work would be supervised by Agriculture and Interior officials. Countering labor objections that a dollar-per-day wage rate would depress other wages, he noted that the government would be paying for the enrollees' housing and food. Roosevelt also took care to appoint a union official, the Machinists' Robert Fechner, as director of the CCC.

From the start, Roosevelt was determined to maintain a direct personal interest in the program. On April 3 he sketched the organization chart of the CCC, misspelling Fechner's name but underlining that he wanted "*personally* to check on the location scope etc of the camps." He was particularly anxious to purchase southern pinelands and land on the coastal plain of the Carolinas and southeast Texas, where there was no Forest Service land: "the wider the distribution of federally owned and developed forests, the wider will be the public interest and education in regard to the importance of organized forestry." Land there would also facilitate moving camps to warmer areas in the winter.

But a bottleneck quickly developed as papers for the sites of individual camps piled up on both his and Louis Howe's desks. The army came to the rescue and streamlined the procedures for registering enrollees and dispatching them to the army-run camps. By the first of July, 274,375 young men—not women—were enrolled, and 1,300 camps were in full operation. Howard Lange, a young ROTC officer just completing medical school, recalled being summoned to Fort Leavenworth to help process young enrollees from Kansas City and St. Louis. They then set off on an epic train journey over rusting, little-used tracks with an engine that could take only half the train at a time up their final climb. Once there, they found they would have to cut a five-mile road through the forest to reach the selected campsite on top of a mountain. A blunt major told them, "How do you expect me to make a road and build a camp on six days' notice. I had orders to select a camp site not build one. We have no funds to hire men to build camps. You'll have to build your own with what skilled labor you have in your outfit." They would have several boys, he said, who had had experience as carpenters or apprentices. They would have to live in tents until the barracks were built but "You have plenty of tents, and the summers are long down here." The major warned Lange to be careful of contaminated water, especially since "springs are full of rattlers, and the creeks have their quota of cottonmouths." It was a simple matter of "You have your orders, it's up to you to carry them out."

Despite the initial culture shock to the young enrollees, many of whom had never seen the countryside before, no New Deal program commanded such universal support. The young men reforested denuded slopes, cut woodland breaks to prevent forest fires, built roads to give better access to the forests, demonstrated soil-conservation techniques to farmers, and worked on irrigation and flood-control schemes. Fifty years later they still recalled their efforts with pride and affection. Here was a relief program that uniquely satisfied both urban and rural politicians, so much so that it was the only agency Congress later attempted to safeguard from budget cuts. Even Senator Ellison D. "Cotton Ed" Smith of South Carolina, a vitriolic critic of most New Deal social engineering, later rhapsodized that the CCC was "the most marvelous piece of legislation that had been enacted during the present or preceding Administration."

Relief

"FDR did not," according to William Bremer, "come into office with a blueprint of federal relief plans in hand." There was, after all, already substantial federal spending on unemployment relief. Congress had accepted that private and local resources were inadequate to cope with the effect of mass, rather than temporary, unemployment. A reluctant Hoover had signed the Emergency Relief and Construction Act in 1932. Although social workers and progressive critics decried the fact that the bill provided for RFC loans, rather than grants, and required states to sign a "pauper's oath" to demonstrate that their financial resources were exhausted, by the time Hoover left office, 80 percent of spending on unemployment relief was paid for by the federal government. States had to apply regularly for renewal of their loans and demonstrate their wise stewardship of federal monies: as a result, field representatives of the RFC's Relief Division, who were usually experienced welfare administrators, had the opportunity to scrutinize professionally local relief administration for the first time. They could coerce states to set up competent administrations. As Joanna Colcord of the Russell Sage Foundation celebrated in May 1933, "All but four states have now some form of state-wide relief organization, more or less effectively developed; and social workers of training, experience and good professional standards have been brought into positions of influence in more than half of them."

But the appropriation for the RFC would be spent by the end of May. Roosevelt, who had pioneered state spending on relief when he established the Temporary Emergency Relief Administration in 1931, knew only too well how limited state and local resources for relief spending were. In New York between 1929 and 1932, private spending on relief had increased sevenfold, public spending eightfold, yet the minimum needs of large numbers of the unemployed were still unmet. His TERA chairman, Harry Hopkins, had testified to the lame-duck Congress that they needed a separate federal agency that would spend between $600 million and $1 billion: the money should be in the form of grants, not loans, and there should, as with TERA, be incentives to ensure that states met their obligations. Aside from grants that matched local contributions, there should also be discretionary grants to be made by the federal administrator.

The American Association of Social Workers had established a Committee on Federal Action on Unemployment, which had masterminded the lame-duck congressional hearings. On March 7 they sent Hopkins and William Hodson of the New York Welfare Council to Washington to see Frances Perkins. In turn she persuaded FDR to let her meet with Hopkins and the three senators who had led the fight for federal unemployment assistance. Other cabinet members took up the cause, and Roosevelt agreed. When he sent the message to Congress asking for the establishment of the CCC, he indicated that he would need to appoint a federal administrator for relief. La Follette, Costigan, and New York senator Robert Wagner introduced the legislation, which was a carbon copy of TERA in New York. The new agency had $500 million to disburse as grants to the states: half of it matched every three dollars a state spent; the other half could be spent at the discretion of the administrator. The legislation passed on May 12, and Hopkins was appointed on May 19, after a five-minute conversation with Roosevelt, who told him, first, to provide immediate and adequate relief to the unemployed and, second, to avoid politics and politicians.

Hopkins's later pivotal role in the New Deal and in Great Power diplomacy during the war might lead one to think that he was a central figure in the Hundred Days and that his appointment to the new Federal Emergency Relief Administration was inevitable. In fact, Hopkins was not part of Roosevelt's inner circle in New York. In the last nine months of FDR's governorship, Hopkins conferred with Roosevelt no more than a dozen times, on four occasions only by phone. The temporary nature of his assignment on May 19 was evidenced by Roosevelt's telegram to his successor, Governor Herbert Lehman. It was "imperative," said the president, to have someone "immediate on job." It had been difficult to find a suitable candidate for this special work. He "felt Hopkins could get away for a month or two without interfering in your state program."

Hopkins had grown up in small-town Iowa, the son of an improvident harness maker, who aspired to own a bowling alley, and a stern Methodist mother. But Grinnell College, where he followed his sister, Adah, was a hotbed of the Social Gospel and scientific inquiry. Hopkins's classmates, imbued with this ethos of professional social service, included future New Dealers Florence Kerr and Hallie Flanagan at the WPA, and Chester Davis and Paul Appleby in Agriculture. Davis described Grinnell as "one of the most democratic institutions I've ever known." Hopkins left Grinnell and went to be a settlement worker in New York, then was employed at a number of private and state charitable organizations, including the Red Cross in World War I, when he directed relief efforts for servicemen and their families in the Gulf states. As his first wife, another social worker, recalled, Hopkins "always felt very deeply about the fact that there were masses of people who had a terrific struggle . . . for mere existence, and on the other hand there was this extravagance of great wealth and waste. I think he felt that very strongly. And he felt that something should be done about it in our own democracy." Hopkins saw how unemployment, not moral defect, caused poverty. He passionately disliked the demoralizing effect of cash handouts, or dole, and aimed to limit the intrusive and demeaning aspect of private charity casework. What he championed and experimented with, both in private work and at TERA, was work relief: jobs for the unemployed.

Hopkins had become part of a network of social workers and reformers during the Progressive Era, centered in New York, who formed a sort of "interlocking welfare directorate" that would be at the heart of the New Deal. Mostly women, they nevertheless, like Hopkins, tended to be Protestant and middle class, from smaller colleges in the rural areas and smaller cities of the Middle West. As "an active vigorous personality boy," Hopkins rapidly went to the top of his profession in the transitional years before social workers were all professionally trained. He would be president of the American Association of Social Workers in 1923. Directing Red Cross operations in the South, Hopkins developed the informal, results-oriented administrative style that characterized his New Deal relief programs. Former colleague William Matthews recalled Hopkins's frequent and informal conferences with staff as "old-time prayer meetings" characterized by the rapid-fire give-and-take of ideas.

Thirty minutes after he left his May 19 meeting with the president, Hopkins commandeered a desk in the RFC building. To launch a relief program quickly from scratch, he recalled, "was almost as if the Aztecs had been asked suddenly to build an aeroplane." He got hold of state applications to the RFC that had not yet been approved and disbursed $5 million in two hours. The next day he telegrammed state governors to tell them not to wait to send in an application but immediately to telegram in a request. He had neither the time nor the authority nor the personnel to set up a federal bureaucracy. He relied on governors to set up relief administrations like the one Hopkins had operated in New York. But Hopkins was quick to impose federal standards as a condition of loans and grants to states. He pioneered what his assistant Corrington Gill called the revolution in methods of caring for the unfortunate destitute. The reliance on local administrations meant that Hopkins ran up against local incompetence, miserliness, fiscal conservatism, and outright corruption. At the same time, he began to professionalize relief operations. In Washington, the staff, which never exceeded 750, were almost without exception welfare professionals who had never been elected to public office or been attached to political parties. At the local level, young trained social workers, mostly women, replaced the local politicos and elite women who traditionally ran local welfare boards. States and localities desperately needed the money that only Hopkins could disburse. Albeit often grudgingly and under protest, they did what they needed to in order to qualify for assistance. Slowly amateurs were replaced by professionals.

At the end of the Hundred Days, Hopkins's old mentor and charities commissioner from New York, J. A. Kingsbury, noted that:

> Harry is a changed man already. He is a bigger, better and more serious man—he is an older man. With full power and responsibility for the distribution of $500,000,000 he has something of the air of a member of the Morgan firm! I don't mean that he seems cocky, but he has the air of a man who has great power, who is enjoying it, who is determined to use it wisely, and as a dictator, if necessary.

Hopkins dreamed of a welfare system in which every American was guaranteed a measure of economic security. That dream seemed far removed from the America of the time, where the unemployed received a miserable dole or, in even more humiliating fashion, stigmatizing food coupons. Hopkins was determined to change that degrading treatment of the unemployed. With the great power that he had acquired, he would seek, in the long term, to replace the dole and the means test with jobs and social insurance.

Farmers

The Economy Act had been a necessary part of the emergency solution to the banking crisis. The creation of the Civilian Conservation Corps had been an easy way of putting off decisions on major public works spending. The creation of FERA was dictated by the approaching end of the existing RFC appropriation. But the need to do something for farm recovery was pressing and inescapable. On March 8, the Brains Truster Rex Tugwell and the new secretary of agriculture, Henry A. Wallace, convinced Roosevelt that a golden opportunity existed to pass farm legislation before Congress recessed. Roosevelt authorized them to call farm leaders to Washington to draft it.

Over the years, the importance of farm legislation and the visibility of secretaries of agriculture have steadily diminished. But in 1933 the top priority given to agriculture was not surprising. Farming contributed 30 percent of the workforce. The Depression confirmed what Roosevelt had argued throughout the prosperous twenties: there could be no permanent prosperity if agriculture did not flourish. But the economic imperative was even greater in 1933. For FDR advisers such as Rex Tugwell and Mordecai Ezekiel, farm recovery was a precondition of industrial recovery. Ezekiel believed that the farm collapse was responsible for the loss of 6.5 million jobs since 1929. Raising farm purchasing power was a crucial first step to restoring general prosperity.

The political imperatives to act were formidable. Roosevelt owed both his Democratic Party nomination and his general election victory to rural southern and western votes. His supporters expected action to remedy their plight. In the Midwest, farmers displayed their impatience much more forthrightly than did the urban unemployed. They went on strike in the dairy states and violently halted foreclosure sales on the farms in the corn belt. A wry observer noted that the governor of Wisconsin, Albert Schmedeman, twitched constantly. Every time he heard a sudden noise, he thought another cheese factory had been blown up. In the spring of 1933 the Farmers' Holiday Association, under Milo Reno, threatened a national farm strike. Crop predictions for the summer created yet more urgency. Huge carryovers of cotton, corn, and wheat already loomed over the markets, promising low prices. Now crop reports suggested that even more bumper crops were likely in the summer of 1933, threatening absolute disaster for all American farmers.

What made agriculture unique for New Dealers was they had a policy all ready to unfold.

The problem for farm policy makers *before* 1933 was that there seemed no way of adjusting farm production in line with demand. Neither the McNary-Haugen plan, so fervently backed by the farm bloc in Congress, nor the stabilization schemes launched by the Federal Farm Board under Herbert Hoover actually curbed production and thus seemed incapable of raising farm prices. McNary-Haugen supporters seemed to assume that you could simply dump surpluses, no matter how large, abroad, and still afford to support the price of the domestically consumed crop. The Farm Board stored surpluses. Without production controls, these eventually had to be unloaded on an already glutted market, further depressing prices. Exhortations to farmers that they follow their industrial counterparts and voluntarily control production were futile. It was not rational for an individual farmer to cut back on production unless he had some guarantee that his neighbor would do likewise. If his neighbors did not follow suit, and there was no overall cutback in production and therefore no price increase, the farmer who did reduce merely lost money, while his neighbor profited.

But if exhortations to farmers voluntarily to reduce their crops

were counterproductive, how could farmers be compelled to cut
back? What constitutional provision existed to tell them what they
could or could not grow? How could the government police what
happened on millions of individual farms? Prohibition had illustrated that the bureaucracy necessary to enforce a ban on the production of alcohol was too large to be politically acceptable. How
much more impossible to contemplate was the scale of officialdom
necessary to police individual fields and farms?

Agriculture, however, possessed an intellectual establishment—
academic agricultural economists and scientists—who were in-
timately wrapped up in government, either in the Bureau of
Agricultural Economics in Washington or in the federally sponsored land-grant colleges in each state. In turn, these academics
were in close touch with the farmers themselves, or at least the
more substantial ones, through an army of county agents from the
Extension Service, the field service of the land-grant colleges, who
attempted to pass the benefits of the latest research on to the farmers. It was at the land-grant college in Montana that an agricultural economist, M. L. Wilson, squared the circle of effective crop
control without compulsion.

Wilson despaired of the traditional approach of the colleges
and the agricultural research establishment. What was the point of
showing farmers how to grow two blades of grass where one grew
before if the farmers were already producing too much? Wilson did
not believe it possible to lower the costs of wheat production sufficiently to make wheat profitable. Apart from the immediate problem of overproduction, he had at the back of his mind a trip to the
Soviet Union that convinced him that one day the Russians would
organize their agriculture and then flood the world market with
wheat at a price the Americans would never be able to match.
What agricultural economists and scientists had to do was persuade farmers to adjust their production to market conditions. The
Bureau of Agricultural Economics gave the farmers that market
information so that they could plan their production accordingly.

The long-term adjustment in crop production that such planning would entail was always Wilson's ultimate goal. In the late 1930s he would get the chance to set up land-use planning committees to help farmers make those adjustments. But in the short term, Wilson saw no alternative but to cut back on production. The beauty of his Voluntary Domestic Allotment Plan was that it provided both positive incentives for farmers to cut their acreage and a nonstatist mechanism for effective enforcement. Under Wilson's scheme, the government would pay farmers who agreed to reduce their acreage. A farmer was perfectly free to refuse to cooperate. Farmers who participated might share the benefit of any price rise that overall reduction brought about, but they would not receive any government payment. The farmers themselves would enforce their scheme by checking that their neighbors had complied with acreage cuts.

Wilson set about vigorously lobbying farm editors, politicians, and businessmen in favor of his plan. In the summer of 1932 he converted Brains Truster Rex Tugwell and the editor of the most influential farm journal in the country, Henry A. Wallace. They ensured that Roosevelt would include the domestic allotment plan in the all-encompassing campaign speech at Topeka that laid out his farm policy.

It was Wallace whom Roosevelt appointed as secretary of agriculture. Few men had a more profound understanding of farm problems. Wallace's grandfather had established the publication *Wallaces Farmer* in Iowa. His father had run the magazine and become secretary of agriculture under Harding and Coolidge. Young Henry Wallace had been an outstanding agriculture student at Iowa State University. Serious and insatiably intellectually curious, Wallace as a boy had been taught to experiment with plants by George Washington Carver. As a fifteen-year-old he demolished the idea behind the popular corn shows of the period by showing that the seeds from the best-looking ears of corn did not produce the best yields. He was fascinated by genetics and tirelessly pursued experiments in inbreeding corn.

In 1926 he and a few friends established the Pioneer Hi-Bred Corn Company. Their progress was slow. At the start of the 1930s less than 1 percent of corn planted was hybrid. But by 1965 virtually all corn planted in the corn belt was. In the 1990s the giant chemical company DuPont paid $9.4 billion for the company Wallace had established.

A statistician, Wallace wrote the 1920 book *Agricultural Prices,* later described as the first true econometric study produced in the United States. But he also took over the family magazine and fervently supported his father's efforts to secure legislative remedies for the farmers' plight in the unsympathetic Republican administrations of the early 1920s. Henry Wallace blamed Herbert Hoover, with whom the Wallaces had clashed repeatedly as war food administrator and as secretary of commerce, for his father's early death.

Yet the endlessly curious scientist and hardheaded businessman admitted that "fundamentally I am neither a corn breeder nor an editor but a searcher for bringing the 'Inner light' to outward manifestation of this Inner Light . . . most important I shall be seeking an opportunity to find the religious knowledge of the new age." Wallace had an insatiable appetite for spiritual inquiry. He was particularly attracted to Native American and Irish mystics, who proclaimed an immediate and tangible link between the land and deep spirituality. Wallace sought advice from Charles Roos, a Native American priest and corn grower, who encouraged him, in July 1932, to contact Roosevelt. "Yes! Poseyemo says HAW must contact Roosevelt in August and leave his totem in Big Tepee. Feel certain this is a big move on your part. Go After it." Immediately after Wallace took office, the Irish sage George W. Russell (the poet AE) wrote him: "I have been thinking of you holding the casket—the sacred most precious casket. And I have thought of the New Country going forth to meet the seven starts under the sign of the three stars. And I have thought of the admonition 'Await the Stone' . . . who shall hold up the compelling vision to these who wander in darkness? In answer to this question again we welcome you. To drive out the depression. To drive out the fear."

Mystical Wallace may have been; shy and awkward he certainly was. Unlike his father, he could not make small talk with old-time politicians and farm leaders or play poker or chew tobacco. Instead, he would take close associates on long walks in Washington or play tennis. But in taking over at the Department of Agriculture, he was coming home. He knew the department heads but also knew their limitations. He knew what he wanted. He brought in Rex Tugwell as undersecretary and installed Mordecai Ezekiel as economic adviser, bypassing his and his father's old friend Nils Olsen, who he rightly thought would be too rigid to adapt to the new ideas necessary to meet the crisis.

Wallace, Tugwell, and Roosevelt had been won over to the Voluntary Domestic Allotment Plan. But how were they to win over the competing farm organizations, who all had their own competing recovery plans and were deeply skeptical of the unprecedented interference in the individual farmer's right to plant what he liked? One leader referred to the domestic allotment plan as the National Quarreling Farmers Plan.

In the White House they devised the solution on March 8. They would sell the scheme as one that came from the farmers themselves. They would draw up a bill that would incorporate as many of the competing farm policies as possible and then, on the same pattern as the banking bill, grant broad authority to the executive to implement the most appropriate option. Rex Tugwell recalled that

> It occurred to us that the protracted [congressional] wrangling we were dreading might be evaded by an omnibus emergency bill authorizing the proposals being pushed by the competing lobbyists. Decisions could thus be deferred and perhaps altogether removed from legislative bickering.

Successful action, we thought, might smother arguments; and, best of all, we might get to work.

A year earlier, Congress had failed to pass a bill granting similar authority to the Farm Board to choose from among the three policies favored by the leading farm organizations.

On March 10 and 11, farm leaders hurriedly summoned to Washington agreed to the broad outlines of a farm bill. Most were convinced, as they had been by the Topeka speech the previous summer, that their own pet scheme appeared in the bill somewhere. The crucial support came from the Farm Bureau Federation, an organization that had strong support in the South and Midwest and close institutional links with the Extension Service. Its leader, conservative Alabaman Edward O'Neal, had no love for production controls. But his organization had suffered in the Depression, and O'Neal needed a convincing policy outcome that would attract farmers in the corn belt from the militant Farmers' Holiday Association. He calculated that the best way to secure the future of the Farm Bureau and reclaim its membership was to hitch its star to Roosevelt, make itself indispensable to the passage and implementation of farm legislation, and reap the political rewards accordingly.

Wallace was able to announce agreement on national radio on March 10. Feverish drafting enabled an omnibus bill to make it to Congress on March 16. The domestic allotment plan was there. Rental and benefit payments to farmers who reduced their acreage would be paid for from a tax on the first processing of farm products. The self-financing nature of the scheme was a condition laid down by FDR at Topeka: it also was essential to survive the scrutiny of Lewis Douglas. But the domestic allotment was only one of the options. To satisfy advocates of the McNary-Haugen approach, there could be subsidies to farm exports. George Peek, the champion of McNary-Haugen, would also be satisfied by the marketing agreement provision, where, for a particular commodity, the processors would sign an agreement to pay a minimum price to the farmers for their product. The overall aim of the legislation was to raise farm income to parity—i.e., to establish the same relationship between the prices farmers paid and those they received as existed in the so-called golden age of American agriculture between 1909 and 1914.

The drafters hoped the permissive quality of the legislation would secure quick passage in Congress. In the House, the plans were untroubled. Marvin Jones, chair of the House Agriculture Committee, representing Texas and cotton, had little difficulty shepherding the bill through by March 27. After all, its arguments had been thoroughly rehearsed in hearings only a couple of months earlier, in the lame-duck session of Congress.

But the bill stalled in the Senate. The lack of informed popular support for the production controls was exposed.

The proposed bill did little to stave off the threat of foreclosure, which reached record levels in the spring of 1933. States had enacted moratoria to halt foreclosure. Floyd Olson, in Minnesota, had done so by executive order; other governors had called out the National Guard to stop farm sales. Farmers had taken matters in their own hands, with vigilante violence to prevent sales at auction. In late April, farmers in Le Mars, Iowa, would send shock waves through the politicians' ranks when they dragged a judge from the courthouse and strung him up from a tree. Only the intervention of a local newspaperman dissuaded the mob from a lynching.

If the farm bill succeeded in raising farm prices and income, that would not lessen the accumulated burden of debt for those farmers who had been desperately striving to head off creditors. Repayments on debts now, after savage deflation, represented a much higher percentage of a farmer's income than when he had originally borrowed the money. Once again, one expert had studied the problem, devised a solution, and Congress accepted the prescription: Roosevelt had consolidated existing rural credit agencies into a new single Farm Credit Administration, under his

Hudson Valley neighbor and close friend Henry Morgenthau, Jr. It was Morgenthau's adviser William Myers, a conservative farm economist from Cornell, who devised a scheme that was tacked on to the farm bill. Two billion dollars in bonds issued by the land banks would enable rescue loans to be made to stave off imminent foreclosure and then to refinance existing mortgages. The maximum interest rate for old and new loans would be 4.5 percent, and there would be a five-year grace period. In the long run, Myers reorganized farmer-controlled loan associations by reestablishing regional credit corporations and four thousand local production-control associations. Within a year the FCA had made a quarter of a million farm loans and authorized another quarter of a million. By the end of the decade, federal land banks would be responsible for 40 percent of the nation's farm mortgage debt.

Lynn Frazier and William Lemke from drought-ravaged North Dakota wanted a more straightforward remedy. The government should directly underwrite existing loans and inflate the currency. Like so many traditional farm state representatives, Frazier and Lemke saw no need to restrict production; they saw no reason to control the independent farmer, and they sought one-off solutions to the problem of farm prices, solutions that would not involve any increase in the permanent apparatus of the state. Among "some simple and magical moves" they sought was a guarantee of the cost of production, most passionately advocated before the Senate Agriculture Committee, by John A. Simpson of the National Farmers Union. For Simpson it was simple: buyers would operate under license and be required to pay a fixed price to cover the cost of production for the portion of the farmer's crop that would be consumed on the domestic market. "We do not want the farmer restricted in any way but we do want the home folks to pay us cost of production for what they use."

By contrast to this panacea, which would not restrict the farmer's independence, Simpson argued that the domestic allotment plan would need a large, coercive, and costly bureaucracy. It

would require, he told the senators, two hundred thousand employees and an annual administrative budget of $600 million. To Wal-
lace and his advisers, the cost-of-production amendment seemed to
be a classic piece of interest-group politics. Irrespective of the me-
chanics of regulating all farm sales in a supposedly noncoercive
and nonbureaucratic fashion, they believed that to guarantee the
cost of production to farmers without accompanying production
controls seemed to be a guarantee of government funding for ever-
increasing surpluses. This particular agrarian remedy shared all
the defects of the other special-interest proposals for farmers of the
1920s. Farmers would be assured profitable prices year after year—
without any restrictions, adjustments, or any cooperative action.
Nevertheless, the farm state senators, acutely conscious of the
threat of the Farmers' Holiday Association, successfully inserted a
cost-of-production amendment into the Senate bill. Ardent supporter of FDR George Norris from Nebraska led the fight.

Farm state politicians were also attracted to another nonstatist, one-off farm-recovery measure. The question of both farm
income and debt, they argued, could be solved simply by currency
inflation. Proposals ranged from the free coinage of silver to the
printing of greenbacks and were advocated by politicians from the
silver-producing states, such as Roosevelt loyalist Burton K. Wheeler
of Montana, by farm politicians, by economists from Cornell University, and by a well-financed pressure group, the Committee for
the Nation, headed by James H. Rand. Henry Wallace himself
wanted an "Honest Dollar" that would better enable the price the
farmer received in money terms to more accurately reflect the
value that that same money price enjoyed in the 1920s. For Senator Elmer Thomas, from Oklahoma, who skillfully put together the
various inflation remedies into one permissive amendment, the issue was simple:

> For over three years the people of the United States have
> been engaged in war with the forces of deflation.

Through the curtailment of credits and restriction of currency, causing enforced liquidation, bank failures, bankruptcies and hoarding, we have lost from circulation some thirty billions of bank credit or deposit money.

This is approximately one-half the money in circulation when the crash came in 1929.

His amendment, he believed, would restore that money into circulation. It authorized the president partially to remonetize silver and to issue greenbacks. The amendment assembled different inflation options in a permissive form just as the administration was providing for alternative policies in the bill itself. The first thing Roosevelt did was to ban the export of gold. The United States was finally off the gold standard. The linchpin of Lewis Douglas's sound-money policy was knocked out at a stroke. It was, he despaired, the end of Western civilization.

Roosevelt attempted to placate outraged conservatives like Douglas by arguing that he had to accept a modified and permissive inflationary amendment in order to head off a mandatory measure. In fact, the Thomas amendment has never been a mandatory measure. The United States went off the gold standard in the final analysis because Roosevelt was convinced that he had to do something about the domestic price level. He had avoided making unequivocal hard money commitments during the interregnum. In the six weeks since his inauguration he could see that he had taken more money out of the economy than he had put in. Farmers would not wait indefinitely. The farm program would take time to establish itself and even longer to put money directly into farmers' pockets. A measure of controlled inflation promised to buy Roosevelt time.

The concession by Roosevelt on inflation was one of the moves designed to win over Senate critics. To assuage the cantankerous chair of the Senate Agriculture Committee, Ellison D. "Cotton Ed" Smith, who believed the bill would give Wallace "entire over-

lordship" over every farm and processor in the country, the bill provided his favored "cotton option scheme" as an alternative. Grow-
ers could exercise the option of buying stored government cotton if
they reduced their acreage. George Peek, of the McNary-Haugen
battles, was appointed to the new agency to administer the act. His
appointment would reassure advocates of the McNary-Haugen
plan and neutralize any potential criticism from his mentor,
Bernard Baruch, to whom many Democratic senators were indebted. The minds of senators were also concentrated as the day
for a national farm strike drew closer, as the threat of violence in
the corn belt intensified, and as the crops, especially cotton, began
to spring up. As a result, the House conferees were able to stand
firm against the cost-of-production amendment and the Agricultural Adjustment Act finally passed on May 10. Milo Reno called
off the national farm strike.

The eventual passage of the Farm Act, and the concessions
Roosevelt had to grant to ensure success, illustrated the give-and-
take that characterized relations between president and Congress
in 1933. Roosevelt was extraordinarily successful with Congress—
but Congress was no rubber stamp.

FDR had large majorities to work with: Democrats controlled
the Senate 60–35 and the House 311–116. One hundred and
thirty-one of the Democrats were freshmen, acutely conscious of
the dissatisfaction with the status quo that had thrust them into office. Patronage demands on congressmen were even greater than
usual because constituents desperately needed jobs in the Depression and the party had been out of the White House for twelve
years. Roosevelt and Jim Farley, who systematized the distribution
of patronage, made it clear that most appointments would not be
made until after the session was over.

The Republican Party was divided. Conservative Republicans
from the industrial Northeast were early opponents of government infringements on individual liberty in the Hundred Days.
But as many as fifty of the House GOP members and twelve of

the senators were western progressives who supported most early New Deal measures. Four of them—George Norris, Hiram Johnson, Robert La Follette, Jr., and Bronson Cutting—had endorsed FDR in the 1932 election. Minority Leader Charles McNary, of Oregon, was enthusiastic about almost all the Hundred Days legislation. At the end of the session he commented, "Our country is on the upgrade. Industries of every kind are feeling the impulse of better times. The program of President Roosevelt supported by the Congress has inspired confidence and courage, and doubt has given way to doing." No measure gave McNary greater pleasure than the passage of the Farm Act, which he saw as fulfilling at long last the promises of the McNary-Haugen legislation, which he had tried in vain to get Republican presidents to sign. Fifteen Republican senators joined him on the final vote. Thirty-nine Republicans, thirty from the West, supported the Farm Act in the Senate.

All congressmen were conscious that their constituents needed relief in the economic emergency, and what they heard from them was that their representatives were expected to support an overwhelmingly popular president in the drastic measures, especially spending programs, needed to provide that. Nowhere was this constituency pressure more important than in the South, and southerners were at the heart of congressional leadership. In the House, Majority Leader Joseph Byrns was from Tennessee, and the chairs of the Rules and the Ways and Means committees, Edward W. Pou and Robert L. Doughton, were from North Carolina. The key figures in the Senate all came from the South—Vice President John Nance Garner, from Texas; Majority Leader Joseph T. Robinson, from Arkansas; chairman of the Finance Committee Pat Harrison, from Mississippi; and the influential behind-the-scenes operator James F. Byrnes, from South Carolina. FDR had enjoyed easy relations with these men throughout the 1920s; they had been to see him at Warm Springs; ultimately they had backed him for the presidency.

The South and border states also contributed five irreconcilable senators whose states-rights, limited government, fiscal conservatism led them to oppose most of the emergency legislation. Carter Glass and Harry Byrd of Virginia, Josiah Bailey of North Carolina, Millard Tydings of Maryland, and Thomas Gore of Oklahoma expressed in no uncertain terms their opposition to what they saw as the statism and profligacy of the Hundred Days legislation. They all voted against the Farm Act.

But for most southern Democrats in Congress, their friendship with and loyalty to Roosevelt were buttressed by the recognition that the cotton and tobacco South had been devastated by the Depression. They were enthusiastic supporters of the emergency New Deal. The Hundred Days provided them with patronage and public works projects. FDR also attacked their mutual enemies—Wall Street and the public utilities—and did not interfere in the region's racial practices. The Farm Act provided what the farm leaders in their constituencies wanted, and it did not threaten local racial and economic hierarchies. The treatment of black sharecroppers was simply not an issue in the debate over the Farm Act in 1933.

Western progressive Republican Hiram Johnson noted that the Farm Act was based on principles that were incomprehensible and frightening for most congressmen. It could pass (and he voted for it) only because the president wanted it. Roosevelt had made important concessions in the six weeks needed to get the act through. Neither of the congressional agriculture committee chairmen, the one from Texas, the other from South Carolina, liked production controls. But they and the other southern congressional leaders would ensure that the Farm Act was passed.

Implementation

Wallace and Tugwell had hoped to avoid precisely the "legislative bickering" that had occurred. Now they faced the task of choosing between the alternative policy options laid out in the act.

The cause of production controls that Wallace and his closest advisers thought necessary was made more difficult by the appointment of George N. Peek as administrator of the new Agricultural Adjustment Administration. Peek had advocated higher prices for farmers ever since his farm machinery company had failed in the 1920s. He had been the key figure in the fight for the McNary-Haugen legislation. He was both admired and liked by Wallace and M. L. Wilson, by the leaders of farm organizations and by farm congressmen. But he resented the fact that he was not the autonomous head of the AAA in the way in which his one-time friend and business partner Hugh Johnson answered to no one as head of the industrial recovery program. Peek insisted on bringing in his own legal team, since he disliked the radical Ivy League–trained lawyers whom general counsel Jerome Frank brought in to staff the AAA's legal division. These lawyers were brilliant, but they had little knowledge of agriculture and had a desire to protect urban consumers and, later, southern sharecroppers, as well as to raise farm prices. Above all, Peek opposed production controls. Instead he advocated marketing agreements with the processors that would raise the price they paid to farmers. He saw no reason to cloud the negotiations of those agreements by trying to restrict the price rises, which the processors might pass on to consumers, or by gaining access to the processors' books to monitor compliance with the agreements. He was equally happy to subsidize farm exports to overseas producers at whatever cost. At first, it seemed as if there would be a policy deadlock. But Peek's friend Chester Davis, an agricultural editor and farm organization man, was brought in to head the Production Division of the AAA and break the deadlock. Davis appointed advocates of production control to head the individual commodity sections. M. L. Wilson, for example, headed the Wheat Section. They soon secured the farmers' consent to implement production-control schemes in the major commodities.

Would the program be costly and bureaucratic as John A. Simpson and the opponents of production control believed?

There was an immediate test of the AAA's effectiveness and cost. Policy makers were confronted by such huge carryovers in cotton and the potential surplus of hogs that they decided not only to sign farmers up to reduce future production, but also to destroy existing production. They aimed to plow under 10.5 million acres of cotton and slaughter 6 million piglets. To sign up more than a million cotton farmers in less than a month, the AAA turned to the one organization with representatives in every county—the Extension Service. Now the AAA would use these agents to administer the crop-destruction program. They signed up the farmers to contracts in which they agreed to plow under their cotton and reduce their acreage in the future. The agents then used committees of the farmers they worked with—usually the leading farmers in the community—to check compliance with the program. Throughout the South mules that had been painstakingly drilled to walk between the rows of cotton were now made to trample down those same rows.

The same pattern of using county agents and local farmer committees was followed in all the production-control programs. As a result, the bureaucracy at the AAA never rose beyond three thousand. The cotton program in 1933 paid out $112 million to the cotton farmers and cost only $2.8 million to administer ($2.1 million of which went to the costs of local committees). Simpson and the other anti-statist critics of production control could not have been more wrong.

Critics would condemn the New Deal farm program for restriction and scarcity financed by a regressive tax on consumption and for handing over the control of the program to large farmers who, in the South, would discriminate ruthlessly against black and poor white sharecroppers. Henry Wallace himself was painfully aware of the waste of destroying crops when "Only the merest quarter turn of the heart separates us from a material abundance beyond the fondest dream of anyone present." But during the Hundred Days, the overarching priority was remedying the plight of all farmers large or small. Crop destruction and production controls were self-confessedly temporary remedies; they were adapting in agriculture what was standard practice in industry. The farm policy makers believed that by putting money into the hands of farmers they would help stimulate domestic demand and overall recovery. After all, they were dealing with the largest sector of the American economy. Only later did economists such as Mordecai Ezekiel come to realize that farm recovery could not by itself create the demand to bring about industrial recovery. Rather than solving urban problems by solving the farm problems, New Deal agricultural planners came to appreciate that the equation worked the other way around: the long-term solution to the farm problem lay in increasing urban demand. But they were not alone in their original misperception. The other farm policy alternatives in 1933—cost of production or currency inflation—simply aimed to put more money in the farmers' hands. They made no pretense of solving the problem of how urban America could afford to buy what American farmers could produce.

The New Deal put its faith in grassroots democracy. In the absence of a police state, a dramatically interventionist program such as production control had to rely on the consent of the farmers themselves. In the economic emergency of 1933 the AAA turned to the only organization that had the staff to implement the program, the Extension Service and its county agents. It was inevitable that the farmers the agents turned to would be the larger and more influential farmers, who would make the program work. In the South the hierarchical local social structure meant that sharecroppers and tenants, especially African Americans, would not necessarily be protected. But the protection of tenant farmers in the South under the crop-control measure was simply not an issue in the Hundred Days. Only Senator George Norris even hinted at it during the Senate hearings. The policy alternatives that aimed single-mindedly to raise prices for commercial farmers also did not address the issue of the rural poor in the

South. The realization that there was a problem of rural poverty in the South that would not be solved even if farm prices revived was first uncovered by New Dealers themselves in the summer of 1933. Harry Hopkins and his field representatives in FERA, who had assumed that the main demands on them would be to relieve the plight of the urban unemployed, discovered in the South that they had to confront a rural-relief problem as well.

Free-market critics have lambasted the AAA. Production control was ineffective. If it secured price rises, it was at a disproportionate cost to the taxpayer. Increased yields offset acreage controls. Drought made controls unnecessary in most of the wheat states. Government payments privileged larger farmers at the expense of the poor, it subsidized inefficient farmers, and encouraged them to stay in high-cost production, which world market conditions made uncompetitive. But in the Hundred Days a free-market noninterventionist approach was simply not possible politically. What would the farmers have done in the summer of 1933 if no money had come to them? They would have been driven from the land, but where would they have gone in the absence of any jobs in the nonfarm sector? In the drought states, the payments for participating in production-control programs were often the only income the farmers received when their crops were wiped out. The production-control program of the New Deal was a workable short-term solution that enabled desperate farmers to stay on the land.

Nevertheless, despite the tireless efforts of the AAA and the local committees, arranging for compliance with contracts to be monitored and for checks to be paid out was slow. By mid-September many cotton farmers still awaited payment. Payments in Kansas were made in January, not in September, as had been hoped. As a result the most enduring farm policy device of 1933 was not in the Hundred Days at all but later in September. Desperate southern politicians put pressure on FDR to authorize price-support loans. Roosevelt created the Commodity Credit Corporation, which would lend money to farmers at a fixed price for their cotton, which they would then store with the government. These were nonrecourse loans: if the price of cotton rose, farmers would take their cotton out of storage and benefit from the higher price; if it did not, they would simply leave the cotton with the CCC and not pay back the loan. When crop-control payments were slow to reach wheat farmers later in the year, the program was extended to wheat. Five years later, in the Farm Act of 1938—the defining piece of agricultural legislation for the next half-century—price-support loans were at the heart of the measure.

Chester Davis, looking back on the efforts of his fellow AAA administrators in 1933, concluded: "I think it would have been impossible for human ingenuity at that time, based on the experience we had and what we knew, to come up with a better program than we did. I don't know what better we could have done." Given the emergency conditions and desperate plight of farmers in 1933, the need for speed, the lack of a national administrative apparatus, the need to secure the consent and support of the farmers themselves, it is difficult to dispute Davis's judgment.

Nevertheless there were unanticipated consequences of the emergency measures of 1933 that neither Henry Wallace nor Chester Davis welcomed. Policy makers such as M. L. Wilson and Mordecai Ezekiel in 1933 had been anxious to avoid special-interest politics aimed simply to increase farm prices without any adjustments in farm practice. But to secure political support for, and implementation of, production control, the New Deal created, or strengthened, commodity interest groups. In 1933 these groups applied pressure for what New Deal farm policy makers wanted to happen. As agriculture recovered, so these interest groups became less dependent on government and more independently powerful through their close ties with key congressional lawmakers. In the long run, the links they established both with Congress and in the commodity sections of the Department of Agriculture enabled them to secure more and more special-interest legislation for farmers that was more and more generous to the agriculture sector. It also enabled them to block New Deal efforts to plan agriculture more rationally in terms of world market conditions, to expand urban demand through lower food prices, or to aid the rural poor.

FOUR

Industrial Recovery: The Belated Priority

Putting People to Work

"Our greatest primary task is to put people to work," said Roosevelt in his Inaugural Address. But by mid-May little had been done to employ people in the nation's cities and industries. Nothing had been done to stimulate purchasing power or investment in the nonfarm economy or to create new jobs, except for short-term relief for the unemployed and jobs for the lucky quarter of a million people who would work in the Civilian Conservation Corps. Saving the banks and refinancing debts unfroze assets and prevented further deflation but did not put a single person back to work. The Farm Act aimed to stimulate rural demand, but if it worked, it would also increase the prices that workers as consumers had to pay. Currency inflation aimed to help debtors and increase commodity prices but would cut into, rather than increase, wages.

When he came into office, Roosevelt did not appear to think special action was necessary to promote industrial recovery. On March 9 he had asked Raymond Moley to keep an eye on the various recovery proposals that were floating around Washington. But on March 18, when he indicated his legislative priorities to Moley, there was no mention of a public works act or any industrial recovery measure. A month later Roosevelt provided a similar memorandum for Vice President Garner. He had already sent messages to Congress for securities regulation, the creation of the Tennessee Valley Authority, and mortgage refinancing. There would, he indicated, also be bills for railroad reorganization and banking reform. He acknowledged that "there is the problem of a public works bill but it is my present thought that this can be tacked on to one of the other bills in the form of a broad appropriation." Forty days into the Hundred Days, therefore, FDR did not envisage significant industrial recovery legislation.

Yet, on May 17, Roosevelt sent a comprehensive message about industrial recovery to Congress. He called not only for $3.3 billion in spending on public works but also for a massive program of industrial cooperation. American industry, he proposed, would be exempted from the provisions of the antitrust laws and would operate under codes that would regulate wages, hours, and prices and guarantee workers the rights of collective bargaining. He sought to create demand in the economy, restore the profitability of American industry, and so put people back to work.

Historians on the left have seen the driving force behind this recovery program of Roosevelt's as representatives of large consumer-durable manufacturers anxious to choke off an increasing challenge from smaller competitors. The industrial recovery codes were part of a larger New Deal enterprise that would impose higher costs on the smaller firms, which they, unlike the larger firms, could not sustain. But historians on the right have argued that the driving force was the antibusiness, socialistic planners of the New Deal or the regulatory reformers of the Brandeis/Frankfurter school, who thought that business inhibited rather than stimulated recovery. The industrial recovery program, they have argued, was the first of a series of antibusiness measures that delayed recovery in the United States while other countries recovered more speedily with business-friendly policies. Even historians friendly to the New Deal have conceded that the industrial codes of the National Recovery Administration contributed little to recovery and that the inadequate public works spending, initiated too slowly in 1933, was a major missed opportunity to inject sufficient purchasing power into the economy to kick-start recovery.

In fact, no area demonstrated more vividly the diverse sources of policy and ideas in the Hundred Days. These policy initiatives came from congressional progressives, from trade association spokesmen, from organized labor, from academic economists, from self-appointed publicists who temporarily grabbed the spotlight, and from the cabinet. They did not come from the president and a single-minded group of advisers. Roosevelt's industrial recovery program sprang, on the one hand, from pressure that left him no alternative but to put proposals forward and, on the other, from a remarkable openness to a wide variety of unorthodox ideas.

Public Works and Sharing the Work

In the spring of 1933 there was no shortage of ideas to kick-start the American economy and create new jobs.

Public works spending in the United States already had a long history and served distinct but linked purposes. The first was simply to put the unemployed to work locally. The second was to foster economic stabilization. Government spending could compensate for, and correct, downswings in the economy by stimulating demand for heavy industry. Finally, public works could foster long-term economic development by delivering investment in the infrastructure. After World War I, economists argued for a public works reserve that could be called up when the economy turned downward.

In the 1920s Senator Robert Wagner from New York had argued for a federal public works board with $150 million that would almost automatically be activated to prime the pump whenever the economy slowed down. Herbert Hoover always accepted that there was a legitimate role for the federal government in major public works. During the Depression, he urged state and local governments to speed up the initiation of planned spending projects in order to hasten recovery as he had successfully done in 1920–1921. He also recognized a role for federal spending on great national projects that developed the economic infrastructure. However, Hoover was prepared to support only self-liquidating public works projects that would pay for themselves in the long run.

In 1932, Wagner was joined by western progressive allies such as Robert La Follette, Jr., of Wisconsin, Bronson Cutting of New Mexico, and Edward Costigan of Colorado in advocating at least $5 billion in public works spending. Hoover was reluctant to jeopardize the budget, but he was under intense pressure to spend money on unemployment relief. If he was going to have to agree to more spending, his preference was for countercyclical spending on public works rather than on relief. The Emergency Relief and Construction Act of 1932 provided $1.5 billion in loans to states for self-liquidating public works and $322 million for national projects, such as the Hoover Dam, in order to stimulate heavy construction. A new division was created in the Reconstruction Finance Corporation to administer the program, but by the end of December 1932, only $147 million in loans had been approved and only $15.5 million spent. Only $6 million had been spent on national public works.

As the congressional progressives watched the early New Deal unfold, they considered unemployment relief a mere palliative. It would be public works spending that would stimulate demand for heavy industry and put people back to work. La Follette himself thought $9 billion in new spending would be needed to secure recovery.

Few politicians had looked at the problem of unemployment more closely than the Wisconsin senator. He drew on not only the commitment of his father, "Fighting Bob," to progressive taxation, regulation of utilities, and defense of organized labor but also Wisconsin's tradition of applying academic expertise to legislative issues. Acutely aware in his own state of both urban and rural distress, La Follette, through his committee hearings, had exposed the utter inadequacy of relief efforts under the Hoover administration. But he recognized that adequate relief was not enough, and he had consistently pressed for major public works spending to revive the economy.

On May 8, 1933, La Follette, Costigan, and Cutting introduced a bill authorizing $6 billion in public works expenditure. Public works had congressional appeal. Whatever their views on fiscal rectitude, congressmen would greedily eye the prospect of projects bringing jobs and money into their own districts. As a recovery measure, public works, like currency inflation, also offered the chance to kick-start the economy without new bureaucracies and controls. Unlike currency inflation, it did not appear wide-eyed and radical.

Roosevelt was keenly aware of the pressure for public works spending. He heard from the building unions of the American Federation of Labor, from the construction industry, and from the congressional progressives. Within his own ranks he heard both from those advisers who wanted business to take the lead in recovery and, conversely, from those who doubted business's ability to act in the national interest. For all these groups, public works spending was a device that did not interfere with the prerogatives of private industry. But Roosevelt had little liking for it. Spending on the scale necessary to make any impact threatened to derail the economic program in which he had invested such political capital. Furthermore, he thought it impossible to devise and engineer enough appropriate projects to spend that amount of money. On April 26 he had asked Harold Ickes to chair a group to consider public works proposals. When the group went to the White House on the twenty-ninth to present a bill for $5 billion in public works spending that Secretary of Labor Frances Perkins had prepared, Roosevelt asked "what public works were there that would call for the expenditure of such a large sum?" Presented with a list drawn up by contractors and architects, he dismissed the projects in New York one by one. He doubted that there were more than $1 billion worth of socially useful projects in the whole nation.

Another "start-up" program enlisted congressional support. Why not spread employment by sharing the work among the workforce? The American Federation of Labor enthusiastically backed a measure to mandate a thirty-hour workweek. The textile and clothing industries, in particular, saw the value of controlling production by that route. Hugo Black, the liberal Alabama senator, sponsored a bill in the Senate that passed on April 6, and a month later the bill looked likely to pass the House. Black believed the thirty-hour week would create six million extra jobs. To head it off, Roosevelt authorized Frances Perkins to introduce a more flexible alternative, which provided for minimum wages as well as maximum hours but also boards for each industry with broad powers to allow exemptions.

Businessmen reacted with horror to this expansion of government power and potential regimentation, and the Perkins bill was quickly dropped. In any case, sharing the work was scarcely a kickstart to growth. At best, it would increase the number of people in employment, but not the overall purchasing power of the workforce. Indeed, it might not even share the work around very much, since surveys suggested that part-time employment had already reduced the average workweek to thirty hours. Business, critics argued, would resist wage increases in the absence of increased demand or would pass the higher costs on to consumers and further decrease purchasing power.

Industrial Self-Government or Government Planning

In addition to these "start-up" schemes, plans for a more sustained boost to purchasing power and industrial profitability were being hawked around Washington. In different departments and in Congress, teams of economists and lawyers, often ignorant of the existence of one another's activities, were trying to draft plans for some form of industrial self-government that would enable business to cooperate in order to check the deflationary downward spiral.

As a presidential candidate in September 1932, Roosevelt had already shown some awareness of what his Brains Trusters had been trying to convince him: that modern corporations could not simply be dismantled. Instead, he argued in a San Francisco speech that new tools of control were required that would make management more accountable and ensure that the right investment, pricing, and wage decisions were made, enabling America's consumption capacity to match its production capacity. In a memorandum on legislative priorities after the November election, Adolf Berle had told FDR that the second priority after farm relief needed to be industrial stabilization: "Necessarily this involves at least a limited set of exemptions from the Anti-Trust Act."

The guarantee that they would not be prosecuted under the Sherman Antitrust Act was the crucial factor for businessmen who wanted to cooperate in measures for industrial rationalization and stabilization. In the 1920s, representatives of "sick" industries such as coal and textiles and natural resource industries such as lumber and oil had called for stabilization measures. They all suffered from destructive competition that led to a large number of small operators increasing production and cutting wages and prices in an effort to maintain a competitive edge. The Cotton Textile Institute had taken the lead in launching a drive to limit the hours their machines ran. Similarly, in oil, the American Petroleum Institute sought to curb the overproduction that sprang from the opening of the East Texas oil fields. The most vociferous advocate of suspension of the antitrust acts had been Gerard Swope, of the consumer-durable manufacturer General Electric. He had rather different concerns. GE had a vested interest in price and cost stability, since the level of investment required for electrical manufacturing made long-term planning essential. Nor could GE's own programs of welfare capitalism for their workers—workmen's compensation, employee pensions, and unemployment insurance—be sustained unless their competitors were forced to meet comparable labor standards.

In 1933, banker Fred Kent and Brookings Institution economist Harold Moulton, together with personnel manager and former congressman Meyer Jacobstein, drew up proposals for industrial codes where business would cooperate to sustain prices, employment, and wages in return for exemption from antitrust prosecution. Such codes would prevent price and wage cuts. The confidence they would give employers might encourage them to invest and finance expansion. But Kent's team envisaged a more direct stimulus to the economy: the government would either underwrite business losses or make loans to cooperating businesses to enable them to invest and finance expansion.

These ideas aroused Senator Wagner's interest. The German-born Wagner represented the new breed of urban politicians. He saw government providing the services and protection for lower-income immigrant workers in the city, rather than the city machine providing largesse for those urban voters on a piecemeal and informal basis. In the 1920s he had advocated public works as one of the measures to stabilize the economy to avoid cyclical unemployment. But he had also worked with union leaders such as Sidney Hillman, representing low-wage garment workers in New York, who wanted to try to eliminate the competitive pressures in their industry that led to sweatshop conditions. In 1933 Wagner knew that the thirty-hour-week bill was unsatisfactory and was doomed to defeat. He did not think that public works spending on its own would meet his recovery goals. He saw the virtues of the industrial stabilization packages, but he also wanted greater protection for workers, so he enlisted the help of labor economist W. Jett Lauck and Pennsylvania mining congressman Clyde Kelly. They represented the United Mine Workers, who were willing to allow coal operators to fix minimum prices and set production quotas in return for guarantees of collective bargaining. Lauck, former secretary to the National War Labor Board, had worked with the union on an agreement in 1924 to protect the unionized section of the industry against the cost-cutting southern mines. These ideas were later expanded into the Davis-Kelly bill to stabilize the coal industry, which would allow a national coal commission to control prices and production. The crucial quid pro quo for this protection of the employers was a guarantee of the workers' right to collective bargaining. Up till then, there had been few restraints in the United States on determined anti-union employers. In 1932 the Norris-LaGuardia Act restricted the use of court injunctions in labor disputes, but mass unemployment stopped even the strongest union from protecting its members. Wagner and union leaders hoped that protection of the right to collective bargaining, not just in coal, but across the major industries, would give workers the same confidence to organize and protect wage levels that exemption from the antitrust acts would give employers.

Eventually, the administration had to intervene. Ray Moley, who held the watching brief for all industrial recovery proposals, recognized the need for action after the collapse of the administration alternatives to the thirty-hour-week bill. James P. Warburg held a similar free-floating role in the Hundred Days because of Roosevelt's affection for him, his financial contacts, and his friendship with Lewis Douglas. Warburg was familiar with the self-government ideas of Swope and Henry I. Harriman, president of the United States Chamber of Commerce, who was a close friend of Warburg. They encouraged the Wagner group to push forward, and by April 25, the group had drafted a bill that called for antitrust suspension and for codes in the public interest industries that would regulate wages and hours and provide for collective bargaining.

For advocates of industrial self-government, the problem was the catastrophic fall in prices caused by excessive competition. For others the problem was the reverse: the artificially high prices caused by monopolies. Some members of the administration, particularly Rexford Tugwell and Jerome Frank in the Agriculture Department, were skeptical that business could be relied on to act responsibly. The roots of the Depression lay not just in excessive competition but also in the behavior of unaccountable corporations, who had set prices excessively high and had unnecessarily hoarded their profits rather than channeling the gains of productivity into higher wages. Oversavings had led, therefore, to underconsumption. To offset the effect of the resultant lack of purchasing power, government, not businessmen, would have to make decisions about production and labor standards. Although there was a good deal of intellectual support for government planning of the economy, and admiration of apparent Soviet planning successes, there was little idea how such government direction would work in practice. Even Tugwell did not appear to advocate centralized overhead government planning; rather, he seemed to envisage some form of a national industrial council to exhort businessmen to more responsible behavior. Centralized planning was simply not an option in the emergency of 1933: the government lacked both the information and the trained bureaucracy to have any hope of imposing coercive planning. Nevertheless, Tugwell persisted in his view that "the government really ought to take over immediately large blocks of paralyzed industries. At the very least, it ought to take them on lease."

Tugwell was a lightning rod for criticism of the administration. His earlier academic writings, his skepticism about the profit system, his early visibility in the New Deal, and his willingness to articulate his ideas with great panache made him a symbol of socialistic planning to many businessmen and conservative newspapermen. His prolific and lucid accounts of the New Deal have retrospectively exaggerated the prospect of government planning in 1933. In fact, the best that advocates of greater government-inspired discipline in the economy could hope for was to provide government licensing of corporations. These provisions were in the drafts prepared by Tugwell and Frank's group, which coalesced around Undersecretary of Commerce John Dickinson: they gave greater potential for government to dictate and impose decisions on industry. But in reality, the proposals coming from the more articulate advocates of planning differed little in substance from those emerging from the more self-conscious supporters of business-government cooperation.

In the crisis of 1933 the most powerful model of industrial mobilization available to policy makers was the experience of the War Industries Board, chaired by Bernard Baruch, in World War I. The WIB had given industry its head to determine its own price and production policies free from the antitrust threat, and business had triumphantly succeeded in meeting the formidable needs of the wartime economy. No one championed that model more vigorously than General Hugh Johnson. An army officer who had served mainly in the Philippines and on the Mexican border, Johnson had helped prepare the Selective Service Act and organize the draft in World War I. He then served as liaison officer between the War Department and the War Industries Board. WIB chief Bernard Baruch employed Johnson after the war and acted as his mentor. As soon as Roosevelt was nominated in 1932 in Chicago, Baruch, who always liked to be on the winner's side and to impress presidents, made Johnson available to help the Brains Trust. Early in the Hundred Days, Johnson had pressed a public works program and industrial reemployment measure on Raymond Moley in order to match the stimulus the New Deal was giving to agriculture. When Roosevelt appeared to sanction controlled inflation, Johnson was determined to find an alternative policy toward recovery and immediately returned to his WIB experience. At Baruch's suggestion he tried out his ideas on a private meeting of businessmen in Washington to mobilize support.

Moley had worked with Johnson on the Brains Trust and shared his conviction that large concentrations of economic power were inevitable and that antitrust action was futile and retrogressive. He gathered together all the current drafts of industrial recovery legislation, threw them down on Johnson's desk, and gave Johnson the job of producing a draft of his own, bringing in railroad lawyer Donald Richberg and Tugwell to assist him.

By May 4, briefed on these drafting efforts, FDR was prepared to alert the United States Chamber of Commerce to the proposals to increase wages, eliminate unfair competition, and secure the cooperation of industry as a whole. By May 7 he was prepared to tell the nation in his second fireside chat that a new partnership between government and industry was needed. He praised the example of the textile industry in its efforts to eliminate the effects of excessive competition. On May 10, representatives of the various drafting groups finally met at the White House to come to an agreement. A month earlier, James Warburg, surveying the various recovery proposals, had suggested a conference whose purpose "would be substantially to lock the conferees in a room until they agree on a uniform point of view as regards the . . . major issues." Essentially Roosevelt followed that advice and left the protagonists to reach a detailed final agreement.

The bill retained the main features of the Wagner and Dickinson drafts, but while it had a $3.3 billion public works appropriation, the provision for government loans had been eliminated. For too many congressmen and Brains Trusters, government loans smacked of the discredited "top-down" approach of the Reconstruction Finance Corporation under Hoover. They noted that the government had been prepared to lend money to banks and railroad companies but not for the relief of the unemployed. But by taking out the loans provision, they took away the most direct method of stimulating private investment and the creation of new jobs.

Another crucial decision concerned the number of industries to be covered by the code. Wagner and his group had planned codes just for the major industries. As Jerome Frank recalled, "Their idea was for a small number of codes related to major industries. The idea that mattress makers, barbershops and the like would have codes—no one thought of that." However, Johnson fatefully insisted that the codes should cover all industries. On May 17 Roosevelt sent the bill to Congress. At the suggestion of congressional leaders, he left Congress itself to find the $230 million in taxes that he insisted would be necessary to pay interest and amortize sinking funds on bonds for the public works spending.

The Alternative Philosophy

The whole philosophy of the National Industrial Recovery Act ran counter to a profound tradition of antimonopoly sentiment in the United States, manifested most obviously in the Sherman Antitrust Act. The Sherman Act was a blunt and, therefore, often ineffective weapon against monopoly, but Woodrow Wilson's New Freedom had offered a more sophisticated vision under the intellectual influence of the Boston lawyer Louis Brandeis. Large corporations were the product not of natural economic forces but of financial manipulation and abuse. They needed to be broken up, but there was no point in breaking them up if unchecked competition simply resulted in monopolies being re-created. There needed to be permanent government regulation to prevent monopolies from resurfacing. In the 1930s, Brandeis, now a Supreme Court justice, eschewed direct political exposure, but he made his views known to Roosevelt and his advisers through go-betweens such as Felix Frankfurter of the Harvard Law School. Brandeis was committed to large-scale public works, but he had not softened his views on large corporations. Tugwell went with Henry Wallace to meet him: "Most of our talk concerned industrial philosophy: he arguing that bigness is always badness, I maintaining that bigness needed only direction, submission to discipline." Tugwell shared with Brandeis the belief that monopolistic concentrations of power in the economy had contributed to the Depression, with their rigid and excessive prices and their failure to redistribute income and restore purchasing power. But where Tugwell favored controlling the corporations, Brandeis and his followers argued for the restoration of free-market conditions, coupled with reforms to eliminate financial and banking malpractice.

Brandeis and his followers were not, as Moley and Tugwell alleged, irredeemably nostalgic, yearning for an America of "small proprietors, of corner grocers and smithies under spreading chestnut trees." Neither were they automatic opponents of all big business. They accepted that a steel company needed to be large as a natural consequence of technology. They saw less need for a soup maker such as Campbell's to be a large national corporation. They did not have a naïve faith in antitrust prosecution: rather they favored strict financial regulation and progressive taxation as nonbureaucratic measures that would secure and administer a reformed American economic structure.

Brandeis and Frankfurter, who had placed so many young lawyers in the burgeoning New Deal agencies, had little part to play in the drafting of the NIRA. Frankfurter himself put more stress on "a public works program of large proportions than any other because they will unquestionably put men to work." He argued there was "little or no convincing proof that the Sherman Act had either caused or intensified the depression." Nevertheless, he was prepared to go along with antitrust exemptions: if business felt more confident because of that exemption, then they might bring forward investment and employment schemes. However, he feared that business might instead pursue a policy of scarcity and high prices. The codes had to protect labor standards. "The labor clauses at once assume a commanding importance as part of any industrial code." Frankfurter tried to get written in to the legislation the requirement that the secretary of labor initiate and give final approval of the labor provisions of any code. Despite his failure, he was confident that labor's interests would be protected by the right administrators in the NRA.

Frankfurter may have doubted the adequacy of the labor provisions of the act, but they were entirely too far-reaching for many businessmen. The National Association of Manufacturers, as Tugwell noted, "has gone off the reservation and are calling their whole membership to Washington to fight it—because of the labor provisions." To NAM, the bill gave the president too much power to impose codes. What the businessmen worried about were the higher costs that the NIRA would impose. Whereas advocates of the bill wanted higher wages to create more consumer purchasing power, businessmen, represented by NAM, argued that higher wages in advance of recovery would cost jobs, not create them. NAM also wanted to retain their freedom to deal with workers as they had traditionally. They secured committee approval of an amendment proposed by the increasingly conservative labor attorney Donald Richberg that glossed over the guarantee of collective bargaining to emphasize that workers could not be required to join any particular organization. Alerted by United Mine Workers leaders, George Norris of Nebraska mobilized other congressional progressives to defeat what they considered to be a validation of company unions on the floor of the Senate.

Antimonopolists in Congress were a much more powerful force in 1933 than the National Association of Manufacturers. The proposals for antitrust exemption alarmed progressive western Republicans such as William Borah of Idaho and some southern and western Democrats, notably Huey Long of Louisiana. Suspicion of eastern corporations and concern for "the little man" was a potent political concoction. Their concerns were not assuaged by Wagner's arguments that the codes were designed to protect small businesses against the predatory practices of large corporations. Borah secured Senate passage of an amendment to outlaw any code provision that allowed "combinations in restraint of trade, price fixing or other monopolistic practices." But the final version of the bill, which as many as eighteen antitrusters and progressives opposed in the Senate, only provided that codes should not "promote monopolies or monopolistic practices." The bulk of the hostile votes on the final act came from conservative eastern Republicans. The bill passed on July 16.

Implementation

The National Industrial Recovery Act contained something for almost everybody—which is why such a stark reversal of traditional government policy could secure majority support in Congress. Code exemption from the antitrust acts pleased businessmen; codes of fair competition promised large firms protection against the chiseler and small firms protection against predatory big business; codes and government licensing offered possibilities to advocates of planning; guarantees of collective bargaining presented opportunities to organized labor. The codes satisfied those who favored industry-government cooperation, but those who were skeptical of that cooperation could at least be satisfied with the promise of economic expansion engineered by public works expenditure.

Like the Agricultural Adjustment Act, the Recovery Act was in essence an enabling act—which policy options and emphases would be followed, which groups would be satisfied, would depend on the way the act was administered. But three crucial decisions had already been made that shaped the way the National Recovery Administration would operate. The first was the victory of Hugh Johnson over Wagner and his group, who wanted to restrict codes to the major industries. The second decision was the elimination of loans to business. Apart from public works spending, there was now no direct incentive to business to increase investment and create new jobs. The third crucial decision was made by Roosevelt on the day he signed the bill into law. He decided that the recovery agency and the public works program should be administered separately. Hugh Johnson assumed he would run both the National Recovery Administration and the new Public Works

Administration. But Roosevelt split the jobs. Johnson was to run the NRA, but the secretary of the interior, Harold Ickes, would run the public works program.

Donald Richberg recognized how many supporters of the act were unenthusiastic about the industrial codes and were reassured by the public works proposals. He warned that "If industrial control leads off, with public works as a secondary, incidental part of the program, it will be difficult to avoid violent opposition from those now clamoring for public works who might swallow a somewhat 'fascist' proposal to get their 'democratic' measure of relief." Giving the administration of public works to Harold L. Ickes meant that "industrial control" would "lead off" before there were significant amounts of new money pumped into the economy.

At the age of fifty-eight Secretary of the Interior Ickes saw the chance of being in the cabinet as an unexpected opportunity. He had fought for many years in Chicago in support of reform candidates in the Republican Party. Most of the time his efforts had been unavailing. Part of a coterie of progressive academics and social workers whose hero was Theodore Roosevelt, Ickes, like his close friend Senator Hiram Johnson of California, shared an admiration for TR's championing of conservation and despaired of the way the Republican Party had developed in the 1920s. Ickes blamed the powerful conspiratorial forces of big business and corrupt machine politicians for his perpetual defeats. In particular, he blamed the utility companies, whom he had battled in the 1920s in Chicago over municipal control of transportation. He had married into wealth, and that wealth had enabled him to survive as a reasonably prosperous lawyer during the Depression. He had a natural sympathy for the underdog. Briefly he was president of the NAACP in Chicago, and he soon became the most vocal champion of civil rights in the New Deal. He had also, as a result of his friendship with reformer John Collier, founded the Chicago Indian Rights Association. He would make Collier the commissioner of Indian Affairs. Collier would seek to replace the traditional federal Indian policies of assimilation with policies that sought to promote grass-roots democracy on the reservations and to preserve, rather than destroy, Native American culture. Ickes had supported the James Cox–Franklin Roosevelt Democratic ticket in 1920, and in 1932 he organized Western Independent Republicans for Roosevelt.

Ickes had lobbied ferociously for a cabinet post. But Roosevelt, anxious for a western, pro-conservation appointment, had first turned to Hiram Johnson and Bronson Cutting. Only after they rebuffed his offer did FDR turn to Ickes. After a lifetime of combatively supporting losing causes, Ickes had finally hitched his star to an electorally successful politician. He rewarded Roosevelt with a fierce loyalty and hero worship that always overrode the repeated snubs that fed Ickes's persistent paranoia and envy of rivals.

There were sound reasons to give a new program that would spend unprecedented sums of public money to the incorruptible and persnickety Ickes, who was incurably suspicious of both businessmen and politicians. In time he created a remarkably graft-free and efficient public works empire that permanently enhanced the infrastructure of the nation. What was much harder for him to do was to spend money quickly. Setting up a brand-new national organization of engineers and architects was no small task. There were logjams as Ickes failed to delegate sufficiently and as lawyers battled to scrutinize and approve contracts. Inevitably, spending focused on projects that were already in the pipeline and in states where the construction industry was important. Disproportionately, early spending was on roads (because the projects were small and started easily), on military projects, on states such as California, New York, and Pennsylvania, and on dams and flood-control projects in the South and the West. As early as August, critics turned on Ickes for his slowness in starting up the Public Works Administration. Secretary of War George Dern also noted the lack of new money in the program. "This program contains a lot of camouflage. This is not $3.5 billion of new works. We are trying to fool the American people with $3.5 billion which we haven't got." Economist Charles Roos concluded in his survey of the NRA, "A fraction of the NRA appropriations were allotted by the end of 1933 . . . at the end of one and a half years the PWA was able to spend at only one half of the rate which its progenitors had expected to attain in its first six months." In that first six months, critics said Ickes had spent only $110 million of the $3.3 billion allocated in the Recovery Act. Critics were unfair to Ickes. They underestimated the scale of the task of launching a massive public works program. In fact, by January 1934, Ickes had spent $2 billion of the $3.3 billion appropriated, despite what Roos claimed. Apart from Robert La Follette, no politician in 1933 supported the scale of public works spending that could have engineered a quick recovery, and the state capacity to launch those projects quickly simply did not exist.

Public works spending was therefore not going to be a "quick fix" that would put people back to work speedily and give Hugh Johnson time to negotiate the codes that would enable long-term recovery to be on a sound footing. Instead Johnson had to rely on the codes themselves to be an engine of speedy recovery. Could the codes create new jobs immediately?

Here Johnson was handicapped by his own insistence that all American industry be codified. Even the hard-driving restless Johnson could not sign up all of American industry to codes overnight. When he recognized that he had set himself an impossible task, and when recovery did not occur immediately, he resorted to a gigantic propaganda drive to increase wages and limit hours. Employers were urged to sign the president's Reemployment Agreement, a blanket code that provided for a thirty-five-hour workweek and a forty-cents-an-hour minimum wage for industrial workers. Cooperating employers displayed the symbol of the blue eagle and proclaimed, "We Do Our Part." Johnson aimed to recapture the wartime spirit of cooperation and modeled the campaign on the wartime drive to sell liberty bonds. He was also aiming to stimulate the same coercive community pressure for conformity that had been so successfully invoked during the war. Anyone who cheated on the agreement would be subject to the full wrath of an aroused citizenry.

In August and September almost unanimous press backing and mammoth parades offered some hope of success. But public opinion was in fact no sanction against a determined noncooperator. If total demand was not increased, appeals to the goodwill and public spiritedness of American businessmen to keep prices down and wages up were likely to be no more successful for Hugh Johnson than they were for Herbert Hoover, or would be for later presidents such as Lyndon Johnson and Gerald Ford.

The burden of securing recovery therefore fell back on the codes. The need for speed in the summer of 1933 meant that the codes could not be imposed on American industry but would have to rely on the voluntary consent of the businessmen if they were to be put into operation quickly. The idea that the government would impose codes through the licensing powers of the Recovery Act, favored by the advocates of planning, was never seriously entertained. The decision to put faith in businessmen's desire for self-regulation reflected in part Johnson's personal preference born of his World War I experience, and in part the advice to Johnson that the NRA could not withstand a challenge to its constitutionality in the courts. Above all, the government had neither the staff nor the information to impose conditions on American industry. Whereas the AAA could draw on a disinterested bureaucracy in the Bureau of Agricultural Economics and in the land-grant colleges who had acquired a vast amount of information about how American agriculture actually operated, the NRA had to staff itself from scratch. As a result, it had to ask businessmen themselves, just as the War Industries Board had done sixteen years earlier, to come to Washington to run the program.

It was no surprise, therefore, as the codes were negotiated in the summer of 1933, that businessmen achieved most of the goals they had set for themselves. The codes provided a series of price-fixing and production-control devices that some businessmen had long wanted to implement but that the threat of antitrust prosecution had so far inhibited. Wage and hours provisions did little to stimulate mass purchasing power or increase employment. They made little difference to existing wage levels and did little to share the work in the way congressional supporters had hoped. In industry after industry, the employers were well organized, they knew what they wanted, and they had a monopoly of information about how their industry worked. The government could not hope to compete: its representatives were either already sympathetic to business requests or inexperienced and uninformed.

The only effective lever available to the government to extract concessions from business was the promise of exemption from antitrust prosecution. But that lever was effective only in atomized industries where excessive competition was the problem, such as cotton textiles, the first industry to sign a code. In industries such as steel and automobiles, dominated by a few major corporations, the offer of antitrust exemption carried little weight. Here the major corporations already exercised sufficient control over production and prices. What industrialists were determined to prevent was not overproduction but unionization, which might mean they would lose control of their costs by having to pay higher wages.

Consumer and labor representatives were even less well equipped than the government to counter business influence. Frankfurter's initial fears about the lack of authority for the secretary of labor over labor provisions were fully justified. His subsequent complacency that the presence of Donald Richberg, railroad labor lawyer, as Johnson's general counsel, and of Leo Wolman, Columbia University economist, on the Labor Advisory Board would safeguard labor's interest was unmerited. In some industries, such as coal, unions took advantage of the promise of Section 7a of the act to guarantee the rights of collective bargaining. John L. Lewis used the banner of 7a to encourage workers to join the United Mine Workers. In such industries, labor had some influence on the codes. In most industries, it did not.

Business dominance of the code-drafting process naturally progressed to business dominance of code administration. The deputy administrators, key figures in each code, were men usually in sympathy with the idea of business self-regulation. The code authorities were often the industries' own trade associations. In many instances they controlled the statistical information by which their performance might be assessed. Few authorities had consumer or labor representatives on them.

In time the NRA itself would determine clear policy guidelines on issues such as minimum prices, price fixing, and the meaning of 7a for union organization. First, a National Labor Board and then a National Labor Relations Board attempted to hammer out a body of labor common law that defined union rights and attempted to proscribe a whole series of unfair labor practices by employers. The NRA's Research and Planning Division began to acquire the independent information that could be used to challenge the assumptions and arguments of the businessmen.

But in the summer of 1933 the NRA simply did not have the time to establish these clear objectives. There were too many codes to be negotiated. In the end the NRA negotiated 546 codes. Such regulation generated paperwork and bureaucracy that could exasperate the head of Armstrong Cork, the largest producer of bottle corks in the country, whose firm alone operated under thirty-four different NRA codes. It imposed a disproportionate burden on small businessmen, who also found themselves forced to violate codes in order to compete with their larger competitors, who dominated the code authorities. It placed an impossible burden of enforcement on the NRA, whose Compliance Division would have by the end of 1933 a backlog of ten thousand complaints of code violations. A vigorous enforcement policy would inevitably mean the politically undesirable task of using the full weight of government to prosecute a large number of small businessmen. On the other hand, a failure to enforce could, and did, lead to the total break-down of some codes. The large number of codes also contained a time bomb for the administration. They inevitably covered industries whose relations to interstate commerce might strike the courts as distant. There would be little doubt that the steel industry was in interstate commerce, but would the Supreme Court think that the five hundred small stores in the New York poultry industry also were? Two years later the court would rule that they were not and would knock out the entire NRA. In that decision, the court also vindicated those who had always been wary of testing the constitutionality of the Recovery Act by ruling that the code-making process had involved an unacceptable delegation of power by the executive to the legislature without adequate policy and procedural guidelines.

Whose Industrial Recovery Policy?

The domination of the NRA by businessmen has led to its being seen as the epitome of both "corporate liberalism" and the fundamentally conservative thrust of the Hundred Days. Deprived of the opportunity to solve the inevitable crisis of overproduction by seeking markets abroad, leaders of America's most influential corporations sought, as they had done in the Progressive Era, to harness government regulation to sustain their hegemonic control of the American economy and defuse any radical threat to their power. Government-sponsored cartelization would maintain their monopolistic control of the economy, protect their market share, and avoid any radical redistribution of resources to workers. The most recent exponent of this view, Colin Gordon, does not argue that a monolithic corporate elite created the NRA, but he does argue that the NRA, like the Wagner Act and the Social Security Act later, was driven "by the competitive anxieties of business interests." The NRA was a major part of New Deal policies that "were essentially business-friendly measures in progressive clothing."

Both the origins of the Recovery Act and the experience of the NRA challenge this interpretation. It was not leaders of America's largest corporations who provided the stimulus for the Recovery Act. Aside from some of the major oil companies and an isolated voice like Gerard Swope, it was not representatives of the center firms, the large corporations in industries such as steel and automobiles, who demanded federal sanction of business regulation in 1933. Major steel and automobile companies already exercised quasi-monopolistic control over their markets. It was middling- or smaller-size firms in textiles, in the Kansas oil fields, or the small retailers fighting the chain stores who saw their salvation in codes of fair competition. It was academic economists who had been investigating excessively competitive industries such as the New York garment industries and the labor representatives from sick industries such as coal who backed their call for regulation. It was politicians committed to raising mass purchasing power who were most involved in the drafting of the legislation. The giants of American industry were simply not involved. The National Association of Manufacturers opposed the NRA from the start, and NAM was the representative not only of small firms but of middling-size steel interests run by heavy-industry leaders such as the Du Ponts and General Motors.

Right-wing historians have argued, indeed, that the NRA was a profoundly antibusiness measure that imposed higher wage costs ahead of recovery, forcing businesses either to squeeze their profit margins, accept losses, or raise prices. The real purpose of the bill "was not business recovery but increased employment . . .": the latter was intended to come at the expense of the former. If some businessmen nevertheless supported the NRA, they were, critics argue, either misled by Harriman and Swope or convinced that codes and self-regulation were the least objectionable alternatives. They acquiesced in the Recovery Act because they feared that the options available at the time might be worse. They were alarmed by the moves to currency inflation, by press reports of the activities of antibusiness Brains Trusters flocking to Washington, and by the traditional antitrust rhetoric of midwestern, southern, and western congressmen.

This grudging acceptance, rather than positive promotion, of industry-business-government cooperation would last only as long as recovery came and the cure was better than the ill. Business self-regulation may have, because of the circumstances of the emergency of 1933, triumphed in the NRA. But most businessmen took no pleasure in such a triumph. It was not only resentful small businessmen who vociferously came to oppose the NRA. Enlightened businessmen, welfare capitalists who have been seen as the archetypal corporate liberals anxious to manipulate the NRA to promote corporate stability, soon expressed first their reservations, then their outright opposition to the NRA. They feared that, despite business domination of the codes, the NRA might become an effective restraint on business's untrammeled right to manage its own affairs and stimulate both bureaucratic and labor power. Since the NRA failed dramatically to increase business turnover and profitability, they saw no reason to trade off marginal improvements in economic stability for the potential hazards of government intervention. Their subsequent hostility highlighted how few businessmen had been positively in favor of business-government cooperation in the first place.

Did the New Dealers miss a radical opportunity in the Hundred Days? A bolder and more expensive public works program might have been more effective in kick-starting the economy in the summer of 1933, but the government did not have the resources or the expertise to launch quickly the projects that might have injected sufficient extra spending to make a quick and dramatic difference in employment. A more consistent monetary policy might have adjusted the price levels without injecting the uncertainty that the experiments and confusion over inflation produced. But it is unclear that business confidence could have been that easily restored. Concentration on codes for a few key industries might have enabled the government to secure greater protection of labor standards and consumers in the codes. But it is unclear that such codes would have generated extra jobs. It is certain that the New Deal lacked the essential electoral mandate, the congressional support, but above all the state capacity to embark on the centralized planning of the American economy in 1933. Even as committed an advocate of planning and industrial discipline as Rexford Tugwell acknowledged that. What the government attempted with the NRA was the microeconomic management of the economy without the tools that would make the implementation of microeconomic policy possible. If the New Deal was to achieve industrial recovery it would not be through the NRA.

FIVE

The Progressive Impulse

The New Deal as it was developing during the Hundred Days was an emergency response to the crisis of the Depression. Measures to reopen the banks, regulate agriculture, relieve the unemployed, and control industry would not have been considered had it not been for economic collapse. All these measures aimed at economic recovery. Most of them, given the need for speedy implementation, relied on the cooperation and consent of bankers, farmers, and businessmen. Some were ephemeral, and in some cases their institutional legacy was to be short-lived.

When, however, Roosevelt discussed priorities with Raymond Moley on Saturday, March 18, the goals he dictated included passage of bills relating both to the Stock Exchange and to Muscle Shoals in Alabama, where the government had built a dam and a nitrate plant. These measures to regulate the issuing and sale of stocks and shares and to establish the Tennessee Valley Authority were reform proposals whose roots long predated the Depression. They drew for their inspiration on reformers prominent during the Progressive Era and they aroused the hostility, not the cooperation, of the business community. They left a deep imprint on American society, even if the principal beneficiaries and the long-term consequences were not necessarily the ones anticipated by the proponents in 1933.

The Origins of the TVA

The Tennessee River winds for 650 miles through four southern states. In the 1930s the valley's two million isolated inhabitants were among the poorest people in the nation. Their farms were too small to be viable, and each spring flash floods removed yet more of their topsoil. Nowhere was the river more unmanageable than at Muscle Shoals, Alabama, where over a distance of thirty-seven miles, a series of rapids caused the river to drop by almost the height of Niagara Falls. During World War I, the federal government, anxious to eliminate its dependence on Chilean imports for nitrates explosives, constructed two nitrate plants of its own at Muscle Shoals. Electricity for these plants was to be supplied by a water power plant built at a nearby Alabama Power Company installation, and the Army Corps of Engineers started work on a dam farther upstream to control floods and provide hydroelectric power.

Yet, at the end of World War I, only one of the nitrate plants was in operation, and the dam was not completed. The Republican administration aimed to dispose of surplus war property as quickly as possible. Henry Ford, alert to the competitive advantages of a monopoly supply of cheap power and the possible relocation of his industrial plants, seized the opportunity and offered to buy the nitrate plants for $5 million and to lease the power plant for a hundred years, provided the government constructed another dam and power plant. Ford won the enthusiastic support of southern politicians by promising to manufacture cheap fertilizer at the nitrate plants. After all, fertilizer was desperately needed to improve the region's depleted soil. Newly elected Alabama congressman and future New Deal supporter Lister Hill enthused that Ford's offer was the most "generous offer ever made by a citizen to his government." Alternative proposals for the uncompleted facilities proposed to lease them to private enterprise, almost certainly the Alabama Power Company.

The vigilance of one man, the chair of the Senate Agriculture Committee, Republican George Norris of Nebraska, halted the rapid disposal of the government facility. Norris was a fiercely independent, western progressive Republican. His preoccupation with democracy and efficiency made him a fierce opponent of corruption and the spoils system and gave him a deep-rooted suspicion of corporate power, especially as it impinged on farmers, industrial workers, and natural resources. He had an abiding faith in regulation by a disinterested government, close to the people. In drought-ridden Nebraska, control of natural resources such as water was crucial. From the start, Norris saw the high stakes that rode on the Muscle Shoals development—nothing less than the control of the greatest water power site east of the Rockies. He relentlessly exposed the weaknesses of the Ford plan. He argued, on the one hand, that the plan aroused false hopes among farmers since, within the limits of existing technology, fertilizers could not be produced cheaply at the nitrate plants. On the other hand, he argued that the rich automobile magnate was getting an unwarranted subsidy from the government: for $5 million, Ford would secure facilities in which the government had already invested $106 million. When Ford eventually withdrew his offer, Norris turned his attention to the proposals supported by the leading Alabama politicians to lease out the Muscle Shoals facilities to private companies. Norris saw the influence of the "Power Trust" behind these plans. He believed that the great private utility holding companies, under the guiding hand of General Electric, had maintained artificially high electricity prices. Indeed, throughout the 1920s electricity remained a scarce and expensive resource used sparingly by its urban consumers. Private utility companies had resisted efforts to extend electricity supplies to rural areas, especially in the South, citing excessive costs and inadequate demand as reasons for not expanding the supply.

By both sheer force of argument and some procedural legerdemain, Norris managed to keep Muscle Shoals in public hands and to secure the completion by the government of the dam, now named the Wilson Dam, which had been unfinished at the end of the war. Eventually he secured passage of a bill for the public ownership of Muscle Shoals. A government corporation run by a three-man board would oversee the multipurpose development of the Tennessee River, controlling floods and generating electrical power. The corporation would also have the authority to construct electricity transmission lines so that the power generated could be sold not only to the Alabama Power Company but also to other customers such as municipally owned utilities.

Coolidge pocket-vetoed the Norris bill. Hoover, by contrast, vetoed the measure with the stinging rebuke that "This is not liberalism, it is degeneration." But from New York, Franklin Roosevelt applauded Norris's efforts. Public power was one of the touchstones of progressivism in the 1920s, and Roosevelt himself had been attempting to harness the water power of the St. Lawrence River for New York. For years he had been working to secure for the state government the hydroelectric rights on the St. Lawrence. "It is our power," he maintained, and if necessary New York should construct and operate its own transmission lines. Like Norris, Roosevelt was convinced by the Canadian experience that a publicly owned power system could lower rates and act as a "yardstick" by which to judge the rates charged by private utilities.

In 1932 Norris was one of the most prominent western progressives to endorse Roosevelt for president. During the campaign, Roosevelt called for the government to operate Muscle Shoals. Norris was convinced that his Muscle Shoals bill would be passed once again as soon as FDR was inaugurated; this time he was confident it would be signed by the president.

Norris's vision for the multipurpose development of the Tennessee River was his blueprint for all water resource development in the United States—involving flood control, navigation, and power generation. He envisaged "the only scientifically developed" river in the nation. Roosevelt's vision, however, was even broader: the regeneration of an entire region. In January 1933 he invited Norris to join him on an inspection trip of Muscle Shoals and the Wilson Dam. He promised the people of the valley that he would put both Muscle Shoals and the river valley "back on the map." Norris, with tears in his eyes, told the president-elect that his dreams were coming true. Two weeks later, at Warm Springs, Roosevelt laid out his plans to newsmen not merely for flood control and hydroelectric power but for the social and economic planning of the whole valley. He envisaged the rehabilitation of farmers, who would have access to the best farming practice and land use, erosion control, reforestation, resettlement in model communities, and the introduction of small-scale diversified industry. The vast project would relieve unemployment and restore the balance between rural and urban America. For both Norris and FDR the importance of the project was far more than regional: it was the start, said Norris, of "a national program for reforestation, flood control, use of marginal lands and development of power."

The message calling for the creation of a Tennessee Valley Authority that FDR sent to Congress on April 10 was based on the joint resolution Norris had introduced at the start of the congressional session. There was to be a new dam constructed farther up the river, at Cove Creek in eastern Tennessee, and at Norris's insistence, the new authority would be able to construct power transmission lines. Norris shepherded his bill through the Senate, fighting off hostile amendments and adding perfecting amendments as agreed with the White House. The bill that passed the House, however, came from the House Military Affairs Committee and reflected the influence of southern congressmen John McSwain and Lister Hill. They reasserted the importance of fertilizer production, called for the commercial production of fertilizer at Muscle Shoals, and allowed for the leasing of private transmission lines before government construction would be authorized. Wendell Willkie, the dynamic young president of the power company Commonwealth and Southern, representing the utilities, had claimed to the House Committee that there was already an excess of energy capacity in the valley, that his own company already more than adequately served the needs of the region's inhabitants. He was quite happy to buy cheap power produced at the dams, but if the government distributed and sold power as well, then $400 million worth of his company's stock would be wiped out.

In a meeting at the White House with McSwain, Hill, and Norris, Roosevelt decisively came down on the side of the Nebraska senator. In a memorandum for the conference committee, Roosevelt gave his opinion on the disputed items in each section of the bill. Each time, he backed the Norris version, and so that version triumphed in the conference. The act that Roosevelt signed on May 18 provided for only the experimental production of fertilizer and gave unrestricted power to the authority to construct power lines.

In little over four weeks Congress had vested vast powers in a federal government corporation not merely to run an existing government facility and to exercise traditional federal responsibilities for flood control, but also to generate power and to cut across state lines to plan a region's economic life: building towns, relocating farmers, attracting industry. It was possible to pass such a revolutionary bill because the issues had been thoroughly aired for more than a decade and because the government had already constructed the facilities at Muscle Shoals and the Wilson Dam. The Depression did make a difference. The ferment of ideas stimulated by the need to tackle the economic crisis created a climate in which such a sweeping plan could be accepted. The Depression had also weakened and stretched state governments to such an extent that they were prepared to allow Congress to run roughshod over existing state boundaries and responsibilities. But perhaps more than any other measure in the Hundred Days, the TVA owed its existence to the interest and prestige of just two men— George Norris and Franklin Roosevelt.

Organizing the TVA

Could FDR and Norris actually implement the ambitious plans authorized by the TVA Act? A sympathetic former governor, Philip La Follette, watching from Wisconsin, felt that "The Tennessee River is very likely to run onto the rocks." Whomever Roosevelt found to sit on the three-man board would have an immense task to set up and plan an entirely new organization from scratch, equipped to carry out the wide variety of tasks envisaged by the president. A couple of days after Roosevelt had sent his message to Congress calling for the TVA, he had found his man. He summoned the president of Antioch College, Arthur E. Morgan, to the White House and offered him the job of chairman of the yet-to-be-created Authority. Roosevelt had never met the Ohio college president before, and we still have only the sketchiest idea of how the president had even come to hear of him.

Morgan was largely self-taught, yet, without a formal engineering education, he had become one of the leading hydraulic engineers in the country, working first for the government and then for his own successful company in Memphis. He possessed the new professional engineering elite's faith in data and rational solutions. He combined scientific confidence with an archetypal progressive certainty in the righteousness of his own moral and ethical goals. A charter member of the American Eugenics Society, he shared Henry Wallace's confidence in the potential of science to perfect the human species or condition. He came to national prominence when he masterminded the flood-control project designed to prevent the recurrence of the disastrous 1913 floods in Dayton, Ohio. However, his expertise as a dam builder was in flood control rather than hydroelectric development. The dams he constructed in Ohio were dry dams, which stored water only when floods threatened.

Morgan looked forward to establishing a model community based on his own scientific and ethical principles. The opportunity to translate that idea into practice came with the offer to rescue the ailing Antioch College. As president, Morgan set about restoring the college's fortunes through an emphasis on practical education; judicious fund-raising among the wealthy, inventive entrepreneurs whom he admired; and effective self-publicity as a progressive educator through the publication of monthly *Antioch Notes*. Rolls increased, facilities expanded, faculty improved, yet in time, Morgan grew dissatisfied. Neither the students nor the faculty, he believed, shared his ethical vision. In what came to be known as the "Epistle from Portugal" and even in a play, *The Seed of Man, or Things in General*, he bombarded an increasingly bewildered academic body with complaints and demands for higher ethical standards. Faculty, worried by the Depression-induced economic crisis affecting all private colleges, found it difficult to construct a satisfactory response to Morgan's disappointment that the college had not become a "powerful force to remake human society." Morgan despaired that he had to make so much effort to win over the faculty to a viewpoint that was so self-evidently correct. As the hero of his play proclaimed, "Let's find out what is good and call that democracy."

So, it was a frustrated and disillusioned college president who was summoned to the White House in 1933. Morgan had had little enthusiasm for the governor of New York—entirely too party political and insufficiently serious in purpose for his taste—and had voted in 1932 for his fellow engineer, Herbert Hoover. However, for all his faith in science and rationality, Morgan prided himself on his ability to judge a man's character by intuition. His intuition left him in no doubt after meeting Roosevelt that the president was a man after his own heart, a man who shared his vision and his determination not to allow politics to interfere with the social and economic planning of the Tennessee Valley. In Morgan's recollection of the meeting, Roosevelt made "scarcely a mention of power or fertilizer"; instead he laid out a vision "of a designated and planned social and economic order."

With Roosevelt's backing, Morgan threw himself wholeheartedly into the task of helping Norris guide the legislation through

Congress. He was delighted that Norris insisted on explicitly banning political considerations from the appointment process. Morgan himself insisted on an important provision that the Authority should employ its own construction workforce and not rely on the Army Corps of Engineers, with whom Morgan had long been at odds. Once the act had passed and he had been named chairman, Morgan set about recruiting his fellow board members. Roosevelt told him he had to have someone from the South. Norris, for his part, was especially concerned that Morgan appoint a director who was familiar with the wiles and greed of the private power companies. He feared that Morgan trusted the good faith of corporate businessmen too easily. Morgan set his old Antioch administrators on the task of vetting likely prospects, but he was determined to make his own decisions on the basis of face-to-face meetings with the prospective candidates.

To represent the South and oversee agricultural development, Morgan chose the president of the University of Tennessee, despite a warning from one of his Antioch College trustees that Harcourt A. Morgan (no relation) was a "typical college president who manipulated Land Grant College politics without scruple." To look after power, Arthur Morgan selected a young Wisconsin public service commissioner, David Lilienthal, despite danger signals from another Antioch trustee: "Would he be a person to throw monkey wrenches? Type of man who gets lots of publicity—makes rash statements? Starts things? . . . Always shooting his mouth off in a way that is embarrassing." In his interview, Lilienthal laid out his weaknesses and strengths. He was ten years too young (thirty-two years old), not southern, and had no knowledge of the engineering side of the project. To counterbalance these inadequacies, he had an unequaled knowledge of the law of public utilities and a "knowledge of the ways and means of the opposition, namely the electric utilities of the South East."

Morgan's intuitive approval of Lilienthal may have been influenced by the fact that he knew the young lawyer came with the backing of both Roosevelt and Norris. Lilienthal was a product of Harvard Law School and a protégé of Felix Frankfurter. He had cut his legal teeth in Chicago in Donald Richberg's firm, where he represented stockholders in battles with the giant and fraudulent utility empire of Samuel Insull. Appointed by Philip La Follette to the Wisconsin Public Service Commission, he established a national reputation by genuinely regulating the utilities. La Follette's successful conservative Republican opponent in 1932 singled out Lilienthal as one who had "befouled his own nest" and "prostituted public service." Despite the promise of reappointment by the new Democratic governor of Wisconsin, Lilienthal decided that his usefulness in the state was over. His former mentor, Richberg, was now in Washington, and many of his law school contemporaries were also flocking to the capital. Lilienthal leapt at the opportunity to put his ideas into practice on the national stage. When he visited Justice Louis Brandeis he listened seriously to the judge's diagnosis of the Depression and his prescription for recovery. For Lilienthal, Roosevelt's ideas on the TVA "sound very much like Brandeis's ideas applied to a particular area." In other words, the TVA was an enterprise that private capital would eschew because of the lack of profit but "which will render service to the community and at the same time furnish employment to the millions of men who will otherwise be permanently unemployed."

Arthur Morgan's faith in his own intuitive judgment would have far-reaching consequences. He had, in fact, appointed two men with very different philosophies from his own who would collaborate in an alliance that would consistently outvote him on the board, thwarting his utopian vision of the valley's development. But in the Hundred Days, it was difficult to envisage any of the future constraints on the TVA chairman. While the two other board members were closing down their personal and business affairs, it was Morgan who had to make a decision on a host of issues that demanded immediate action. Existing government agencies and the fresh New Deal programs that already operated in the Tennessee Valley—the Army Corps of Engineers, the Geological Survey, the Weather Bureau, the Civilian Conservation Corps, the NRA's Subsistence Homesteads Division—all needed decisions from Morgan. At the same time he had to build up an engineering staff and workforce. He had already had one furious row with Postmaster General James Farley, the Democratic National Committee chairman and the administration's patronage dispenser. According to Morgan, Farley had been "brutally frank and direct" about the allocation of TVA jobs. According to Farley, Morgan had not been so much apolitical as antipolitical, unwilling to recognize that it is "smart practice . . . to avoid antagonizing the men who vote the appropriations."

By the time of the first TVA board meeting, Chairman Morgan had inevitably accrued considerable power. Meeting in a borrowed room in the Willard Hotel in Washington on the day after Congress adjourned, the fledgling organization was operating on a hand-to-mouth basis. As Morgan recalled:

> We hadn't any space yet. There was mail piled around in stacks and in burrowing through this, we would find an important letter from the president, piled under a 3-foot stack of mail; we would find letters from Congressmen, department heads, writing to know what to do about this appropriation or that . . .

At this first board meeting, Lilienthal and Harcourt Morgan, still not full-time for a further six weeks, heard the fully versed chairman outline at length what he had done in areas of which the two board members were largely ignorant. But the board did discuss a letter from Wendell Willkie, head of Commonwealth and Southern, the utility with the greatest stake in the region, asking for a meeting. What was to be the board's attitude toward private utilities? As Lilienthal recalled, "there was to be some difference of opinion as to tactics and strategy expressed as between myself and

Chairman Morgan, with Harcourt Morgan acting as a mediator." With understated foresight, he added, "This will require a good deal of working out."

The TVA was a resounding success and internationally acclaimed as a model for regional development. But for Arthur Morgan, the dispute in that first board meeting foretold the demise of his utopian vision for the valley. Morgan's reputation as an engineer was amply justified: he assembled a highly praised and expert workforce that constructed a breathtaking series of high dams and tamed the river. The first dam at Cove Creek, named for Norris, was constructed in two and a half years instead of the projected four. Morgan's flood-control goals were triumphantly accomplished. But his compelling vision of an "integrated social and economic order" was scarcely attained. The model town of Norris, constructed next to the first dam, was to be the epitome of his new order, with its vernacular housing, a cooperative barn and store, and a small woodworking factory. Morgan's wife attempted to promote handicrafts and convince the residents of the value of whole wheat germ. But local residents resented any form of paternalism, and as soon as the Norris Dam was completed, inhabitants of the model community moved on. There was no work for them in Norris, since the small diversified industries never materialized. By 1947 Norris was largely a bedroom commuter town for Knoxville, and was eventually sold off to a private real estate developer.

Harcourt Morgan and David Lilienthal did not share what they regarded as the chairman's vague and archaic vision. H. A. Morgan revitalized agriculture in the way he knew best. After a lifetime working with the Extension Service, he aimed to collaborate with local community leaders, the Farm Bureau, and the county agents, not to dictate or preach to them. Poorer farmers were the objects, not the makers, of policy. Lilienthal's responsibility and passion was for cheap electricity. He wanted to use the TVA to expand energy production and use, while the private utilities clung to a high-price, low-use philosophy. Chairman Morgan was not interested in power and, as the first meeting indicated, was perfectly content to work with the private utilities, but Lilienthal comprehensively outmaneuvered him politically. Lilienthal made the TVA a gigantic producer of cheap electricity. He fought the utilities in order to build transmission lines across Tennessee, Mississippi, and Alabama. He encouraged rural cooperatives and municipalities to purchase TVA power and he organized low-cost financing to enable consumers to buy the appliances that would boost energy use. In the end the private power companies had to follow suit and lower their rates. To their surprise, they found that demand increased.

By 1945 the TVA had brought electricity to 75 percent of the farms in the valley, compared with the paltry 2 percent connected in 1933. But the TVA did not simply eliminate the daily drudgery of farm life. The TVA was an integral part of the infrastructure of what would be the Sunbelt. Its cheap power would attract industrial giants such as Monsanto and Alcoa and supply the atomic plants at Oak Ridge. While this industrialized South was far removed from the utopian dreams of Arthur Morgan and Franklin Roosevelt, the TVA acted as an inspiration for a new generation of younger southern liberal politicians, who saw the TVA as the model for how the federal government could rescue the South from poverty.

Historians critical of the New Deal have argued that the TVA was "but the opening gun in what was to be a prolonged war by Roosevelt on the investor-owned utilities of the nation." The government subsidized artificially low electricity prices and wiped out the value of stockholders' investments. Two percent of the nation's population was subsidized by the tax dollars of the remaining 98 percent. The TVA flooded more acres than it protected and displaced more than fifteen thousand of the region's farmers. The dams were constructed too slowly to promote recovery. Non-TVA states and counties in the South saw faster economic growth than those areas served by the TVA. Private utilities more than showed that they could meet the region's power needs.

These criticisms of the TVA ignore the fact that the New Deal's rural electrification policies demonstrated that low electricity prices could increase demand beyond anything private utilities had contemplated. The yardstick drove down electricity prices across the region, not just in the TVA area. Far from destroying the private utilities, the TVA showed that a low-price, high-volume policy could profit them. Critics who complained about the displacement of poor farmers have complained at the same time that electrification encouraged marginal farmers to stay on the land, rather than relocate to the manufacturing sector. Rehabilitating these farmers in the valley slowed down the modernization of the economy. What the critics of the TVA fail to acknowledge is that construction of the dams in itself was not meant to contribute to immediate recovery and that the New Deal had ambitious plans, in the end unfulfilled, to extend the TVA concept to other river valleys in the nation. In attributing to the TVA a vital role in the economic modernization of the South, southern politicians in future years had a sounder and broader understanding than some historians of the long-term impact of the TVA.

Regulating the Stock Market

The creation of the TVA was an extension of long-standing conservation battles of the Progressive Era. For all its government ownership, it was essentially a measure that restricted private monopoly control of a natural resource while creating the infrastructure for private agricultural and industrial development. The Truth in Securities Act of 1933 also drew on old progressive battles against private concentrations of power and was bitterly opposed by Wall Street. Yet its aim was also to facilitate, not hinder, private enterprise. "Conservative banking," said one of its main protagonists, Felix Frankfurter, "within its appropriate function has nothing to fear and everything to gain from the Securities Act." Frankfurter was right, and the Wall Street opposition wrong, in their assessments of the act.

The growth of the securities market typified the American pattern of a national industrial economy whose development was not matched by commensurate development of institutions to control its abuses. In the Progressive Era, reformers had distrusted the stock market; Louis Brandeis had thundered that "We must beat the Money Trust, or the Money Trust will beat us." After the speculative booms of the 1920s, economist Gardner Means noted that half of the wealth of the United States was represented by stocks, bonds, debentures, notes, and mortgages, "an intangible form of wealth represented by pieces of paper." Even so, the buyer of horses or secondhand cars had more relevant information to guide his purchases than did the buyer of securities. In the boom conditions of the 1920s, it was estimated that half of the $450 billion in securities issued were worthless. State "blue-sky" laws sounded tough but were, in practice, ineffective, and neither the Stock Exchange nor the Investment Bankers Association demonstrated the will to make self-regulation work properly.

Both President Hoover and many members of Congress believed that speculators had conspired to bring the stock market down by selling other people's stock short to make a profit on their own investment. Investigations by the Senate Banking and Currency Committee made little progress until the lame-duck session when Ferdinand Pecora, a Sicilian-born immigrant who had worked his way through law school to become a district attorney for New York County, used a team of his old legal staff to subpoena vast quantities of records of, first, National City Bank and its investment affiliate and, then, the House of Morgan itself.

With a photographic memory and court-hardened forensic skills, Pecora exposed the chicanery of some of the nation's leading businessmen. Their ability to evade tax by creating paper losses on stock sales; their protection of favored clients with preferential stock sold to them below the market price; their cavalier treatment of small customers whose money they had invested and lost; and their issuing stock to rescue bad loans made by the parent commercial bank—all combined to destroy any lingering public confidence in the integrity of investment bankers.

Roosevelt was committed in his campaign, in the party platform, and in the interregnum to some kind of reform of the issuing of securities and the stock market: to act "when evils are not eradicated by people in the business in which the evil exists." Not averse to a little financial speculation himself, he nevertheless had a patrician and moral distaste for the way men of his own class had betrayed their fiduciary trust at the cost of personal tragedy for so many small investors. Given the plummeting public esteem of the investment bankers, securities reform was a natural priority of the president.

Roosevelt asked the secretary of commerce, the old Wilsonian Daniel Roper, to prepare appropriate legislation. Roper turned to two warhorses of those Progressive Era conflicts, Samuel Untermyer, who had served as counsel to the Pujo committee investigating the Stock Exchange in 1912, and Huston Thompson, one of Wilson's appointments to the Federal Trade Commission, and later its chairman. Untermyer's bill to regulate the stock exchange through Post Office control of the mails was a reworking of his proposals of a generation earlier. As a result, Stock Exchange legislation was therefore quietly shelved until 1934. As for Thompson, Brandeis said that he possessed "every quality that makes a great lawyer except one: 'Brains.'" Nonetheless, when Roosevelt asked Congress on March 29 for legislation, it was Thompson's bill that was considered. He called for all stocks to be registered with the FTC, which could revoke the registration if necessary. Buyers could file civil suits to recover damages, and the directors and the issuers would be absolutely liable. The bill invoked vast powers for the FTC, which could revoke or deny registration for the vaguest of reasons, including if the FTC thought the business unsound or insolvent—but the bill's lack of precision left real doubts as to how effective these vast powers would actually be. Thompson did not want to see any growth in what he already considered a "staggering" army of federal employees. He believed that the law itself would solve the problem at a stroke and would not require complex administration. Sam Rayburn, chairman of the House Interstate Commerce Committee, was unconvinced— "We have passed a lot of laws since we met here on fifth of March, but I do not think we have given anybody that much power yet"— and after four days of expert testimony he was convinced the bill was "a hopeless and unintelligible confection." He called on Ray Moley to help him out.

Rayburn was one of five Texas congressmen who chaired major House committees. Together with former speaker John Nance Garner, they constituted a formidable bloc in the Washington of 1933. In time, Texas would be a hotbed of business anti–New Deal sentiment, but Texas oil, cotton, and cattle were in desperate straits in 1933, and Washington seemed to provide the only solutions on offer.

Rayburn was born in the same year as Roosevelt, but there was little apparently in common between the Hudson Valley squire and one of eleven children of a poor East Texas cotton farmer. Two years painfully eked out at East Texas Normal had given Sam Rayburn a diploma and the chance to teach school. Listening to charismatic Texas politician Joe Bailey, in 1897, had convinced Rayburn that he wanted to be a politician. By 1906 he would be in the state legislature, where he was elected the youngest speaker of the Texas House. In 1912 he set off for Washington as Fourth District congressman, alongside future Judiciary chairman Hatton Summers.

"We were," he remembered, "always so poor at home and everybody worked like the devil. That's what made me determined to try to help the average man get a break." Of all his legislative achievements, Rayburn would be proudest of his role in the passage of the Rural Electrification Act of 1935, which helped to bring electricity to his farming constituents. But from the time he served in the Texas legislature he had been suspicious of the machinations of the railroad companies. Railroads and their rates were important not only to the farmers in his constituency but also to his hometown of Bonham, which was served by rail. He had therefore looked for a place on the Interstate Commerce Committee. By 1933 he was chairman.

Rayburn had never been to Wall Street in his life, he did not study the financial pages of the newspapers, and he owned no stocks or shares. He had once briefly held $1,000 in oil stock but had quickly unloaded it for fear of any conflict of interest. All his savings were in U.S. bonds, land, and cattle. What he shared with fellow East Texas congressman Wright Patman was a populist conviction that the financial institutions on Wall Street were fleecing the average man. What he shared with Houston banker Jesse Jones, now running the Reconstruction Finance Corporation, was a regional belief that eastern banks were starving the South and West of the credit that local entrepreneurs needed to modernize their region. When, on April 5, 1933, Ray Moley passed Rayburn's request for assistance on to Felix Frankfurter, Moley was putting Rayburn in touch with someone who shared his suspicion of those same financial institutions. Moley was inadvertently creating a legislative drafting team that would transform the regulation of the securities market in the United States for the next half a century.

Conservatives saw the hand of Frankfurter in all that was radical and harmful about the New Deal. He served as a convenient whipping boy for an opposition that scarcely concealed its anti-Semitism. Indeed, Frankfurter rivaled Rexford Tugwell in the pernicious influence he was supposed to exercise. In fact, for much of the Hundred Days, Frankfurter was as far removed from real influence on New Deal policy as Tugwell was. Frankfurter owed his reputation to his friendship with Roosevelt. They had known each other in the Wilson administration, when Frankfurter worked for the War Labor Board. Frankfurter had always cultivated Roosevelt, but he did so with even greater assiduity when the governor of New York emerged as the front-runner for the Democratic nomination. Frankfurter's sycophancy knew no bounds as he shamelessly flattered Roosevelt and bombarded him with advice on both policy and people. He appears to have been offered the post of solicitor general, despite the fears of Attorney General–designate Thomas Walsh that he would lose cases in the grand manner. As it was, he preferred to stay in Harvard, to have the ear of the president and to influence the New Deal through the young lawyers who flocked to Washington.

Frankfurter owed his liberal public reputation to his efforts to save Italian anarchists Sacco and Vanzetti from execution, and to his work to establish the constitutionality of labor legislation. He exasperated his senior colleagues in the law school and scarcely concealed his contempt for both its dean and the Harvard president, as well as for conservative Supreme Court judges. What Frankfurter did best was to teach brilliant students brilliantly, to inspire their loyalty and friendship, and then to place them—the very best—with clerkships with Justice Brandeis or with Oliver Wendell Holmes, and all of them with the finest law firms in Chicago and New York. He inculcated in them the desirability of combining private practice and public service. In the Hundred Days their chance came. The New Deal needed legislative draftsmen, and the new emergency agencies needed lawyers to draft the host of contracts and regulations that applied the new government powers in unprecedented ways to states, municipalities, farmers, and businessmen. Frankfurter's pupils were in great demand.

His protégés found niches all over New Deal Washington: Dean Acheson at the Treasury, Nathan Margold at Interior, Charles Wyzanski at Labor, Alger Hiss at Agriculture, David Lilienthal at the TVA. His eyes and ears in the capital were principally those of

Tommy Corcoran, an irrepressible piano-playing Irish American who had moved from the prestigious New York law firm Cotton and Franklin to the Reconstruction Finance Corporation when it was established in 1932. Lurking first at the Treasury and then back at the RFC, Corcoran placed an estimated three hundred to four hundred lawyers in government posts in the next few years. Their prominence prompted conservative laments about the malign influence of these "mischievous cub lawyers." But what these lawyers had in common was their friendship with Frankfurter and a high degree of legal skill, rather than a common political ideology or an agreed-upon policy agenda. In political outlook, there was little in common between Acheson and Hiss; in social manner and intellectual acuity, there was everything. As a passionate Anglophile, Frankfurter hoped that "the best men of the graduating classes of the leading law schools" would act as "disinterested" public servants along the lines of those in the British civil service. Wyzanski recalled their fellow feeling:

> I was not there as a reformer with a program . . . [we were] a level of employees that Washington hadn't previously seen . . . there was an ideal element in most of us . . . Even more intimately than at the Harvard Law School the young men in government in the 1933 to 1935 era ate, slept and constantly talked the topics of their jobs, so that there was constant communication among those people, an energy, an awareness of fresh problems and a feeling that one really counted and that what we did was very important.

Frankfurter himself had little influence over the major pieces of recovery legislation in 1933—he liked neither the NRA nor the AAA. His preferred remedy for the Depression was one he shared with his mentor Louis Brandeis, that of progressive taxation that would produce revenue and curb the excess influence of wealth. A massive public works program would provide the jobs and purchasing power that private enterprise was unable to provide. Like Sam Rayburn, Frankfurter was concerned about the way in which financial leaders had betrayed the trust of their investors and clients. He and Brandeis wanted their activities precisely regulated so that financial markets could operate in a free and open manner, widening, rather than restricting, economic opportunity. Thus, when Moley called on Frankfurter for assistance, the law professor was prepared to drop everything, forget about scheduled classes, and take Benjamin Cohen and James Landis down to Washington to draft a technically competent securities act on Thursday, April 6.

Ben Cohen was working as a corporate lawyer in New York when Frankfurter summoned him. The quiet son of a Muncie scrap iron dealer, Cohen had achieved the highest ever grades at the University of Chicago before moving to Harvard. He followed Frankfurter to Washington during World War I, and afterward went to Paris and London for the peace negotiations. At the behest of Frankfurter and Brandeis, Cohen attempted to represent American Jewry and to try to hold together Zionist factions in Paris and London during the complex negotiations of the postwar Middle East peace settlement. There he met John Maynard Keynes, who was advising the Zionists. Cohen, like Frankfurter, firmly believed in 1933 that the key to recovery lay in government spending on the scale envisaged by Keynes. In New York in the 1920s, Cohen combined his corporate law practice, specializing in corporate reorganizations, with work for the National Consumers League, attempting to draft minimum-wage laws for women that would meet the standard laid down by the Supreme Court in the adverse Adkins decision, which invalidated a minimum-wage law in Washington, D.C., for women and children. During the Depression he became an expert on receivership and on the English Companies Act. Cohen had needed little persuading to go to Washington when Frankfurter summoned him. It was "the center of action and most of us wanted to be part of that action." As he recalled, "For most of us the New Deal years were the best years of our lives."

The young professor whom Frankfurter brought with him from Harvard on the Thursday expected to go back to teach his classes in Cambridge on the following Monday. Instead, James Landis stayed in Washington for four years. Landis was the son of a demanding missionary father in Japan but lost his own religious faith when serving with the YMCA in France and Britain after World War I. He followed a brilliant undergraduate career at Princeton with astonishing success at Harvard Law School, where he reputedly scored the highest average since Brandeis himself back in 1878. Although Frankfurter denied Landis the editorship of the *Harvard Law Review*, he soon became a close friend. They shared their vacations and Frankfurter increasingly relied on him as a co-author. As clerk to Brandeis, Landis extended Brandeis's dissent in the 1926 Myers case on the power of the president to remove executive branch officials from one and a half pages to forty pages. So highly did the justice think of his young clerk that when Landis left to go back to Harvard as an assistant professor, Brandeis wrote to Frankfurter offering secretly to lend Landis $2,000. When the University of Pennsylvania attempted to hire him away, Landis was offered a new chair of legislation. Like Frankfurter, Landis believed the courts took on themselves far too much power in reviewing legislation designed to deal with the abuses of industrialization—economic power should shift from the courts back to the legislatures. Like Frankfurter and Brandeis, he had faith in disinterested regulation; if that failed "there's only one answer, Socialism, Government Ownership. And that's something I don't want to see." Unlike Frankfurter, he had not been impressed by an evasive Roosevelt as governor of New York and had endorsed Al Smith for the Democratic nomination.

On arriving in Washington, Frankfurter left his protégés holed up in a room at the Carlton Hotel with Tommy Corcoran while he went off to the White House. They worked feverishly to produce a draft based on the principle in the English Companies Act of full and fair disclosure. They disliked the Thompson bill in part because it gave so much discretion to a Federal Trade Commission, whose Republican commissioners they distrusted. They thought that the FTC simply did not have the information to decide whether a company issuing stocks was insolvent or not, and they believed that any regulatory exercise of power by the FTC had to be based on a clearly defined standard. By setting out a detailed schedule of information required for registration, they laid down a clear standard by which the FTC would judge whether or not registration statements complied. The key was full disclosure of information, not an assessment of the financial soundness of the company. The FTC had thirty days to decide if the statements did comply; if they did not comply, the stock registration could be suspended or revoked. Liability for supplying false information extended right down from the directors to the underwriters. The Thompson bill made the directors absolutely liable. Cohen and Landis thought it unreasonable to make directors alone absolutely liable for everything, including matters far from their control. Liability, they felt, should be more limited, but it should also be shared by all those who had some role in preparing registration statements—accountants, engineers, appraisers, and lawyers—who would be liable for providing false information. Cohen and Landis hoped that they had drafted a piece of legislation that would eliminate vague discretionary powers and instead "make administration almost a matter of mechanical and compulsory routine."

Rayburn immediately took to the lawyers and their draft: "these fellows were the most brilliant men I ever saw." The acid test came when Wall Street lawyers Arthur Dean, John Foster Dulles, and Alexander Henderson demanded a hearing on the new bill. Landis recalled, "I was 33 years old, new to politics and I was worried that Rayburn couldn't stand the pressure, that he would cave in to this high-finance crowd." When Dulles objected to a provision that was not in fact in the bill, Landis could not re-

sist pointing out that it was not there, and Rayburn asked an em-
barrassed Dulles to point it out. Landis, fearful that he had talked
out of turn, was summoned to Rayburn's office. "I remember how
he glared at me from behind the desk. He ordered me to sit down.
Then he sort of smiled and said, 'I've never seen such shitasses in
my life.' That's when I knew we were on the right track."

Rayburn guided the Landis-Cohen bill through both his committee and the whole House, where with grim relish he declared,
"Today we are forced to recognize that the hired managers of
great corporations are not as wise, not as conservative, and sometimes not as trustworthy as millions of people have been persuaded to believe." As he confided in the House, "This is the most
technical matter with which I've been called upon to deal." In the
Hundred Days the pace of legislative activity was such that few
congressmen could master the details of more than one or two issues. Rayburn and his draftsmen had mastered their bill and no
one in the House was going to challenge Rayburn's word. Debate
in the House lasted five hours and revealed little sign of business
alarm. As Rayburn noted to Cohen and Landis, the bill passed
either because it "was so damned good or so damned incomprehensible."

Meanwhile, Huston Thompson was much aggrieved at the
new bill, a measure that he had been led to believe was simply a
matter of some perfecting amendments. The Senate passed his
bill, but Rayburn, with the backing of Roosevelt and Senate Majority Leader Joseph Robinson, marshaled the House conferees
and secured passage of the House bill on his casting vote. Roosevelt signed the bill on May 27, 1933, and gave the FTC an immediate headache: how to check within a month on every new
stock issue. Landis, without pay, went over to help out.

The Truth in Securities legislation proved to be, as the drafters
intended, "substantially lawyer-proof." Wall Street denounced the
measure and argued that it caused new investment to dry up because firms were reluctant to risk the penalties of inadvertent non-

compliance with its strict provisions. In fact, as one observer noted, the act "has not held up any new financing because there isn't any to hold up." Actually, Cohen and Landis, with their experience on Wall Street, had worked to make their bill (unlike Thompson's draft) compatible with the realities of doing business there. In 1934, Rayburn would summon Corcoran and Cohen back to draft the legislation to regulate the Stock Exchange that established the Securities and Exchange Commission, another example of the ideal of disinterested administrative regulation that Frankfurter and Landis favored so keenly. Later the same team of Corcoran and Cohen would draft the legislation regulating the public utility holding companies. Landis warmed to a president of the United States who proved easier to see than the president of Harvard. He accepted an appointment to the Federal Trade Commission and then to the SEC. Corcoran remained the prime political "fixer" in the administration, and Cohen quietly drafted legislation capable of withstanding the most rigorous constitutional challenge.

Long-Term Reform

In the short term, neither the TVA nor the Securities Act had much effect, and certainly neither made an immediate contribution to economic recovery. Neither measure might have passed had it not been for the ferment of innovative thinking associated with the emergency conditions of 1933, or for the disrepute into which the bills' main opponents—the public utilities and Wall Street—had fallen during the Depression. But the ideas behind the legislation owed more to long-term reform concerns than to the Depression.

However, in the long term, the measures proved to be among the most durable and influential of all the legislation of the Hundred Days. Both measures represented a lasting contribution to the infrastructure of America. The TVA heralded a revolution in the price of electricity and energy consumption, brought profits for the private utilities as much as for the government, and helped kick-start the South into self-sustaining economic growth. The Securities Act and the creation of the Securities and Exchange Commission the following year made an immense contribution to stabilizing finance capitalism in the United States, forestalling for half a century the sort of financial collapses that had character-ized the 1920s. Critics have argued that the 1933 act deterred in-vestment and that the SEC did not improve the rate of return to investors. But they seem to think that a unique period of fifty years of stability in the securities market had nothing to do with the New Deal regulatory framework. Yet only when the Reagan Ad-ministration deliberately softened the regulatory hold in the 1980s did the excesses of the pre–New Deal years return. As in other ar-eas of the Hundred Days, the most bitter opponents of New Deal regulation—the power companies and the financiers—were the most favored beneficiaries of the reforms.

SIX

The International Option

The Nationalist Thrust of the New Deal

Roosevelt proclaimed in his inaugural that "our international trade relations, though vastly important, are in point of time and necessity secondary to the establishment of a sound internal economy. I favor a practical policy of putting first things first." The measures of the Hundred Days confirmed this domestic nationalist priority. The major pieces of recovery legislation—the Agricultural Adjustment Act and the National Recovery Act—were restrictionist measures that aimed to raise domestic prices by curbing production. In order to be effective, restricted domestic production had to be protected from overseas competition. Further, in order to raise domestic prices, Roosevelt had voluntarily taken the United States off the gold standard on April 19 when he accepted the amendments to the Agricultural Adjustment Act, which gave him the power to lessen the gold content of the dollar. Devaluation occurred despite the fact that the Federal Reserve calculated that the United States had sufficient gold reserves to hold off any foreign speculation against the dollar. These measures confirmed that Roosevelt was following the advice of his Brains Trusters that the problems of the American economy were essentially domestic and structural and had to be solved by national, rather than international, means. Lewis Douglas lamented that time and again at the White House he heard the refrain, "We only export five percent of our production, why, then, should we be worried about the foreign market."

Yet during the Hundred Days a succession of foreign leaders, notably from Britain, France, and Germany, came to Washington to discuss a major initiative to end "self-sufficient nationalism" and to seek "International cooperation . . . as the best way forward to national recovery." They all came in advance of the World Economic Conference to be opened in London on June 12. The Roosevelt administration struggled to reconcile its nationalist priorities with its traditional Democratic commitments to fiscal orthodoxy and low tariffs. Roosevelt finally put the priority of raising domestic prices above all other priorities on July 3, when he effectively torpedoed the World Economic Conference and ended the hope that revived world trade would stimulate American economic recovery from outside. How did the Roosevelt administration come to reject the internationalist option?

Plans for an International Conference and Differing Objectives

As the world Depression worsened from 1930 onward, countries increasingly attempted to protect their own interests by erecting protectionist tariffs and by implementing competitive depreciation of their currencies. The more they did so, the more world trade dwindled and the more prices of commodities fell. The traditional informal cooperation of the central banks was incapable of checking this deflationary spiral. Concerted governmental action was needed. Hoover had provided a lead in 1931 by instituting an international moratorium on intergovernmental debt repayments. Britain, the traditional leader in international economic diplomacy, had taken up a low-level State Department suggestion and proposed an international conference to stimulate worldwide recovery. From the start this initiative was bedeviled not only by currency and trade issues but by the question of debts, not just political debts owed by government to government in the form of war debts and reparations but also commercial debts, especially loans by British and American banks to Germany.

In 1931, German conservative leaders, alarmed by Nazi electoral success, had stressed the damage done to German finances by the scale of the reparations that had to be paid to Britain and France following World War I. That summer the German banking system buckled in the aftermath of the collapse of the Austrian Kreditanstalt. The Bank of England initiated a rescue operation to ease the burden of Germany's commercial debts to foreign bankers who had financed earlier rescue packages for the German economy. Standstill agreements froze foreign credits in Germany, but Britain paid a heavy price for the German rescue. By the autumn, Britain had been forced off the gold standard. British invisible earnings had collapsed and worsened the British balance-of-payments deficit. The revelation of the extent of British assets tied up in Germany worsened the situation. To stop the devastating run on the pound, the Labour government could not make sufficiently large spending cuts without splitting the Labour Party. A newly formed National Government came in and immediately went off the gold standard; it then sought to protect its competitive trading advantage created by devaluation by abandoning free trade and instituting general, abnormal, and imperial tariffs in 1931 and 1932. Anxious to protect their commercial investments in Germany, Britain also persuaded France to abandon reparation payments from Germany at Lausanne in 1932.

The British and the French believed that if they lessened their demands on Germany for reparations, the United States would continue the logic of the twelve-month moratorium on debts and forgo the twice-yearly payment of war debts that the British and French had incurred in order to finance World War I. Hoover and his secretary of state, Henry Stimson, may have sympathized with the European position, but publicly they could not countenance an apparently united front of European debtors dictating to their U.S. creditor what they should pay. Congressional opinion remained committed to the line that the Europeans had "hired the money" and should continue to repay their debts. On December 15, 1932, the British made what they intended to be their last full debt repayment, and the French defaulted.

In the fall of 1932, delegates met in Geneva to lay the groundwork for the World Economic Conference. It was clear that Britain, France, and the United States had very different, often mutually exclusive, priorities for the conference. The British wanted a settlement of the war debts issue first and foremost. They were in no hurry to return to the gold standard and forsake the competitive advantage that devaluation gave their exporters. They were prepared to examine the technical operation of the gold standard and to promote central bank cooperation for a cheap-money policy. Similarly, they did not wish to abandon their new tariff protections, especially when it was so difficult to penetrate the Smoot-Hawley Tariff and sell in the United States. As Chancellor of the Exchequer Neville Chamberlain said, "the United States sells to us five or six times what she takes from us. We thought that it was for America to first lower its tariffs, not very substantially, so that we could increase our trade with her."

The Americans absolutely refused to allow the issue of war debts to be on the agenda of the World Economic Conference. Hoover and his Treasury secretary, Ogden Mills, wanted Britain to return to the gold standard. Only when the British had gone back to gold would the United States be prepared to move on the debt question. All they were prepared to offer was the possibility that concessions by the British on trade might lead to the possibility of concessions by the United States on the issue of war debts.

Meanwhile, the French wanted the British back on the gold standard, above all else. The British return would ultimately safeguard the franc. Their own relative economic strength, the French government believed, was due to the gold standard. They had little interest in lowering their quotas on imports and claimed that the Bank of France, by law, could not enter into open-market operations to facilitate a cheap-money policy.

Roosevelt's Confusion

The new president's intentions on debts, tariffs, and the gold standard were unclear. In early negotiations with both Hoover and Stimson, he appeared to think that he would have sufficient authority to persuade Congress to make concessions on war debts in advance of the World Economic Conference. But he refused to tie his prestige to the outgoing president by making a joint appeal to Congress on war debts. His advisers ensured that he insisted on maintaining the distinction between the debts and the conference. Equally, he refused to make a binding commitment to the gold standard and thus tie his hands over currency inflation and a balanced budget. Distrusting the U.S. experts preparing in Geneva for the conference, he set up his own advisory committee, then promptly ignored its advice. He appointed free-trader Cordell Hull to be secretary of state, but then appointed the vigorously nationalist Raymond Moley as assistant secretary of state in charge of issues relating both to debts and to the conference. Moley, who was in any case "constitutionally opposed to orderly and institutional preparation," was already too busy as the president's chief political adviser to master the issues, and he handed over preparation of the conference to a young banker, James P. Warburg, who had strong family ties with the European central bankers. Though Warburg believed in the gold standard, he did not necessarily favor it as fixed at its current rates of exchange. He was scathing both about the "palsied" leadership of Herbert Hoover and about the selfish and blinkered policies of American and European bankers during the Depression.

The forces for a nationalist policy were formidable. Not only did Roosevelt's academic advisers believe in the domestic origins and remedies of the Depression, but traditional farm, business, and labor lobbies also favored tariff protection. Equally potent were the voices demanding some form of currency inflation to relieve both farmers and debtors. It was not surprising that Roosevelt allowed his domestic recovery programs in the Hundred Days to follow the nationalist path.

But there were some countervailing forces in an internationalist direction.

Lewis Douglas, Roosevelt's powerful budget director, passionately believed in the gold standard. It was a concomitant of his advocacy of the balanced budget. The gold standard disciplined its members to balance their budgets and lower trade barriers. Restoration of the gold standard and liberalized trade provisions would enable restoration of investor confidence and revive world trade. This international engine of recovery would complement Douglas's balanced-budget strategy and obviate the necessity for expensive domestic spending programs.

Multinational businesses had a vested interest in opening up overseas markets. Largely capital-intensive firms, such as oil companies and the electrical goods industries, had fared better than many during the Depression. Along with some leading American investment bankers, they saw their long-term future more with the traditionally low-tariff Democratic Party than with the protectionist Republicans. They wanted to break down foreign trade barriers. Their commitment to the gold standard itself was not rigid: like James Warburg, they did not have blind faith in the existing operation of the gold standard; what they wanted was an international monetary system that brought exchange rate stability.

Roosevelt's secretary of state, Cordell Hull, the veteran Tennessee senator, was a traditional southern Democratic advocate of low tariffs. He fervently admired the leadership of the British in the nineteenth century, when they used their international preeminence to promote policies of free trade. Hull had already prepared Reciprocal Trade Agreement legislation that would authorize the administration to negotiate bilateral tariff reductions with individual nations. He would head the delegation to the World Economic Conference and would doggedly pursue the goal of trade liberalization throughout the next decade.

It was not simply conservative businessmen or old-fashioned Democrats who envisaged an international solution to America's problems. Henry Wallace was prepared to support production control and inevitable protection for American farmers as a short-term answer to the overwhelming immediate problems of American farm surpluses. But no one was more convinced than he that the responsibility for the Depression lay with the selfish economic nationalism of both Europe and America during the 1930s. The economy of abundance that he wished to see would depend on an international recovery facilitated by the elimination of protectionist trade barriers. Just as Lewis Douglas believed that the return to the gold standard and international recovery would end the need for large-scale domestic spending programs, so Wallace believed that a new world economic order would also enable him to dismantle the statist apparatus that production control demanded in 1933. Restrictionist economic policies could be accepted only as a temporary emergency solution; in the long term, he believed, the revival of world trade as nations liberalized their trade regimes would eliminate the need for restrictions and controls at home.

Getting Ready for London

After Roosevelt's inauguration, American preparation for the World Economic Conference was chaotic. The main burden fell on James Warburg, but Warburg was also given the brief by Moley of looking over the various recovery proposals coming before the administration. Warburg looked in vain for detailed policy guidelines from the president, had almost no contact with Secretary of State Hull, and could not turn, as he instinctively would have wished, to George Harrison of the Federal Reserve Board because of Roosevelt's distrust of the FRB. Preparations took on added urgency once America had gone off gold, just as the first foreign leaders, British prime minister Ramsay MacDonald and his French counterpart, Édouard Herriot, were about to arrive. Given that the one thing the administration was not going to do under any circumstances was to make concessions on war debts, there was little practical that could be decided in these face-to-face negotiations with European leaders, since it was largely concessions on war debts the Europeans wanted. As one British Foreign Office official noted, the British policy was one of "withholding cooperation on international financial recovery until the war debts question was settled on terms satisfactory to the British government." Given the European determination on the one hand, and American political realities on the other, it was little wonder that an exasperated Roosevelt complained to his friend Henry Morgenthau that "European statesmen are a bunch of bastards."

Nevertheless, the Europeans did want to see some sort of exchange rate stability now that the Americans had devalued. It was left to Warburg frantically to devise some sort of stabilization agreement. He embarked on ever more ingenious ways of engineering a stabilization fund, at one point briefly believing that he had squared the circle—solving the war debts problem, stabilizing the dollar, and providing extra money for domestic spending. At first, the Europeans did not understand the "bunny," as Warburg called his scheme. Eventually, he himself came to realize that it would not achieve what he wanted it to.

On tariffs, Ray Moley delighted in saying, "Let Cordell Hull talk one way regarding tariffs while the army marches in another direction." But in fact, Hull nailed down the visitors in Washington to a tariff truce, an agreement not to raise tariff levels until after the conference. The delegation Roosevelt appointed to go to London was led by Hull and was almost entirely internationalist in orientation but had next to no political influence back home. It set sail with the vaguest of instructions, and an admonition against reaching definite agreements. While the delegation was at sea, Roosevelt let Hull know that he had jettisoned plans to introduce Hull's Reciprocal Trade Agreement legislation in Congress. Meanwhile, Ray Moley laid out limited objectives for the conference in a radio address. "Each nation must set its own house in order and a meeting of all the nations is useful in large part only to coordinate in some measure these national activities."

Chaos in London

When the delegation arrived in London, the first priority was to resume the task of finding a temporary monetary stabilization agreement, which Warburg had been unable to finalize in Washington. Desperate to get some sort of agreement to enable the conference to move forward, the representative of the central banks, together with James Warburg, finally negotiated a temporary arrangement. Britain and the United States would announce their ultimate aim to return to the gold standard. The Bank of England and the Federal Reserve Board agreed upon the level at which they would hold the dollar and the pound and how much gold they were each prepared to lose in order to sustain that level.

To implement such an agreement, Federal Reserve officials needed to know how far the president was prepared to let the dollar fall. They made increasingly desperate appeals to him to find out. But Roosevelt still wanted domestic prices to rise. Even as they negotiated the temporary agreement, Warburg and Governor Harrison had little confidence that Roosevelt would endorse it— correctly, as it turned out. Roosevelt's suspicions of central bankers and his unwillingness to see his hands tied in monetary policy underpinned his warning to the conference that "far too much importance is attached to exchange stability by banker-influenced cabinets." Raymond Moley passed the message on to

Warburg to "tell him [Ramsay MacDonald] it's dead and to bind the wounds." Moley flew to London in a highly publicized move that appeared to undercut Hull and the whole American delegation and inspired the false hope that the conference could somehow be rescued.

To satisfy Roosevelt, the conferees drafted a bland statement that Moley was confident the president would accept. It committed Britain and the United States to a return to gold, but at an unspecified date, and made no commitment to specific rates of exchange or currency stabilization. The statement did little more than make vague mention of good intentions, which had constituted the president's brief to the U.S. delegation before it set sail for London in the first place.

The president was yachting off the New England coast with Vincent Astor and his friends when he received the draft. His only political adviser on hand was Louis Howe, who knew little and cared less about economic policy. Roosevelt angrily cabled London that it was "a catastrophe amounting to a world tragedy, if the great Conference of Nations . . . should allow itself to be diverted by the proposal of a purely artificial and temporary experiment affecting the monetary exchange of a few nations only . . . The fetishes of so-called international bankers are being replaced by efforts to plan national currencies with the objective of giving those currencies a continuing purchasing power . . . Our broad purpose is the permanent stabilization of every nation's currency." This "bombshell" effectively ended any hope of significant action by the London conference. A British government retrospective assessment concluded that the conference's "outstanding achievement" was the establishment of the largest bar the world had ever seen, at which the delegates had opportunity to sample the world's national beverages. The option that had persisted during the Hundred Days of securing American economic recovery through a cooperative international recovery program was abruptly ended. In the bitter words of Neville Chamberlain, "There has never been a case of a conference being so completely smashed by one of its participants."

The Incoherent Aftermath

In Washington before the conference, the chief British economic adviser, Sir Frederick Leith-Ross, had complained that it was difficult to negotiate with Roosevelt because "no-one can foretell which of these two horses [national or international] he is likely to be riding at any particular moment." Roosevelt's message scuppering the London conference appeared to settle that question once and for all. He seemed to have come down decisively on the side of his Brains Trust advisers who believed that America's economic problems were primarily domestic in origin and could be solved only at home. The immediate domestic priority of raising prices had taken precedence over any long-term possibility of an international recovery program.

Roosevelt's message was praised by Keynes and other economists who saw the revival of domestic purchasing power as the precondition for a lasting recovery and who believed that any international monetary stabilization would have hindered, not fostered, recovery. Their praise was predicated on the belief that the decisions paved the way for a planned program of government spending and sensible exchange rate management. In fact, Roosevelt's decision revealed his continued fascination with "quick-fix" recovery devices. He was always searching for a scheme that would secure the price rises, and therefore the recovery, he wanted. Currency tinkering promised recovery without large-scale government spending or substantial statist intervention. He continued to listen to the advice of Cornell economist George Warren, who advocated a "commodity dollar" and attempted to persuade Roosevelt that merely changing the gold content of the dollar would automatically engineer the price rises he sought. In

November, to the horror of both conservative and liberal economists, the president would put the Warren scheme into practice.
This gold-buying policy failed utterly and was quietly abandoned
in January 1934.

European observers and many historians since have condemned Roosevelt's irresponsibility. Roosevelt's "bombshell message" to Europe dashed exaggerated popular expectations of what
the dynamic American president could achieve. British and
French leaders were quick to lay the blame for the failure of the
London conference solely at FDR's feet. Historians have found little to praise in Roosevelt's actions. They blame him for his failure
to make clear policy choices in the months before the conference
and for his amateurish diplomacy. In the negotiations with European leaders before the conference, the president placed too much
faith in his personal charm and off-the-cuff negotiating skills and
too little in detailed preparatory homework. These negotiations,
argued the historian James Sargent, illustrated Roosevelt's "casual
methods, disorderly thinking and ambiguous expression." Too often, Roosevelt relied on personal envoys such as Warburg and Moley, rather than on established diplomatic channels. He undercut
his secretary of state Cordell Hull and bypassed the State Department, as he was so often to do later. He allowed himself to be
swayed by his personal prejudice against the central bankers at the
Federal Reserve and pandered to long-standing popular suspicions
of unscrupulous European leaders. He was too conscious of domestic political constraints and made little effort to educate American public opinion about the issue of war debts. He allowed
himself to be seduced by the harebrained schemes of crackpot
monetary theorists.

For economic historian Charles Kindleberger, the failure of
the London conference was final confirmation of America's responsibility for interwar economic depression. Roosevelt's sabo-
tage of the conference was the last in a series of irresponsible
American actions that constituted America's failure to appreciate

its new role after World War I as the world's leading creditor nation. The Federal Reserve Board's tight monetary policy in 1928–1929, the Smoot-Hawley Tariff, the refusal to understand that Europeans could not pay war debts when they could not sell their goods in the United States, the uncompromising attitude to those debts, and Roosevelt's failure to countenance any form of monetary stabilization all added up to an abnegation of America's responsibility as "lender of last resort." As Kindleberger concluded, only two nations might have led the world to economic recovery. "The British couldn't and the Americans wouldn't."

These damning indictments of both Roosevelt and the United States need to be qualified. It was convenient for European leaders to blame the London debacle on Roosevelt, but in fact no country showed any signs of sacrificing particular national interests in order to facilitate a concerted policy in London. As Patricia Clavin has shown, there was simply not the political will on the part of any of the leading nations at the conference to achieve cooperation. Their perceived national economic interests and their particular experiences of the Depression meant that neither Britain nor France was prepared to make the compromises necessary to secure progress in London.

Britain was determined that action on war debts was a necessary precondition for both central bank action to promote cheap money and for trade liberalization, yet war debts were specifically not on the conference agenda. The National Government had no intention of damaging its apparent recovery by sacrificing the competitive advantages it had gained by going off the gold standard or by giving up the protection afforded by the new tariff barriers it had erected in 1931 and 1932. As Russell Leffingwell of J.P. Morgan observed to Roosevelt, "The British knew enough to go off gold themselves. No doubt it would suit their book to have America back on gold . . . leaving the world to the British oyster."

France, which appeared to have escaped the worst of the Depression, staked all on getting the United States and Britain back

on the gold standard in order to protect the franc against speculative withdrawals. It saw no reason to give up its own import quotas
or to allow the Bank of France to engage in open-market operations in order to facilitate an international cheap-money policy.

Historians such as Barry Eichengreen who have stressed the
damaging effect on the world economy of the gold standard in its
operation between the wars do not see the failure to secure some
form of monetary stabilization in 1933 as the missed opportunity
of the London conference. For these historians the missed opportunity of 1933 was the failure of the leading economies, especially
Britain and the United States, to coordinate reflationary measures.
The best way to halt the deflationary spiral was to escape the "fetters" of the gold standard and to coordinate currency depreciation across the board. Herbert Feis, at the State Department, had
entertained dreams of such a policy but he acknowledged that
those dreams "belonged more to the world of H G Wells" than
that of U.S. Treasury officials. After the bombshell message in
1933, Alexander Sachs of Lehman Brothers suggested to Roosevelt that other countries should be induced to leave the gold
standard, to inflate, to discourage hoarding, and to open up investment and trade. But the suspicions fueled by the London experience militated against any such cooperative international strategy.
It was certainly clear, as Elliot A. Rosen has recently pointed out,
that Neville Chamberlain, as the British chancellor of the exchequer, had no desire for "currency depreciation and public works,"
especially in the British dominions that were primary producers
and whose leaders chafed at the restraints imposed by London and
hankered after an FDR-style reflationary policy. The British were
not going to agree either to any monetary stabilization that threatened the benefits of their own devaluation or to any coordinated
international recovery program that might lead to increased government spending.

The divisions among the British, French, and Americans over
war debts, currency stabilization, and trade ensured that eco-

nomic diplomacy could play little part in the diplomatic response to the growing threat of Hitler's Germany in the 1930s. The London conference confirmed Chamberlain's view that the Americans could not be trusted as far as foreign policy was concerned. To both Chamberlain and the Foreign Office, Roosevelt's foreign policy simply bent to the prevailing wind of ignorant public opinion, and British policy in confronting aggression in the 1930s would have to rely on its own resources, not on the Americans. Germany, by contrast, integrated its economic diplomacy fully into its foreign policy objectives of increasing its military capacity and meeting its territorial ambitions. Indeed Germany was one of the few "winners" at the London conference. The most economically nationalist of all the participants, it nevertheless largely escaped blame for the failure of the internationalist approach. Having declared a moratorium on its repayment of commercial loans, it discriminated in favor of British creditors at the expense of the Americans in negotiating partial repayments, thus securing a sympathetic British attitude and driving a further wedge between London and Washington. Only as Europe lurched to war in the late 1930s would the political need for a common Anglo-American-French front force leaders to accept some economic cooperation.

Yet, despite the nationalist stance of the American government during the Hundred Days and at the London conference, there were the first signs of an emerging economic diplomacy that would culminate in the new economic order negotiated for the post–World War II world at Bretton Woods.

Cordell Hull's role in New Deal diplomacy has been often slighted by historians who argue that he was largely a figurehead bypassed by the personal diplomacy of the president himself or of trusted presidential friends such as Moley, Harry Hopkins, and Sumner Welles. But Hull remained committed to his vision of free trade. Building on the tariff truce that Norman Davis, the veteran of trade and disarmament negotiations, had first proposed at

Geneva and that he had championed in the Hundred Days, Cordell Hull never stopped arguing for reciprocal tariff reductions during the London conference. Presidential policy appeared to undercut him at every turn. Not only did Roosevelt abandon plans to introduce the legislation for Reciprocal Trade Agreements during the congressional session, but Hull's lack of a mandate, the presence of Moley, and the increasingly nationalist policy of the administration all served to whittle away Hull's bargaining power. But he persisted. He exploited Roosevelt's willingness to authorize bilateral negotiations in Washington later in the year. In the short term he made little progress: he was particularly disappointed by the refusal of the British, who were his first and logical target, to take his proposals seriously. The British wanted some prior reduction in high American tariffs before they would contemplate an equal percentage reduction in their own relatively low tariff. But Hull did get the Reciprocal Trade Agreement through Congress in 1934, he secured an Anglo-American agreement in 1938, and he would remain secretary of state until 1944. He would see trade liberalization emerge as a key element in the negotiations of the new economic world order that were started during the war, negotiations driven largely by policy makers who, as low-ranking Treasury and State Department officials in the 1930s, had seen at firsthand the destructive consequences of economic nationalism. They devised a more flexible monetary arrangement than the gold standard and, unlike in 1933, demonstrated the political will to exploit U.S. economic might to dictate terms to other countries.

Just as currency manipulation appealed to Roosevelt in 1933 as a "quick-fix," nonstatist recovery measure, so Hull's Reciprocal Trade Agreement would offer Roosevelt, in the long run, another way of securing economic growth without massive bureaucratic state intervention. The Hundred Days had seen FDR eventually choose the nationalist option, but the door was left ajar for a future internationalist approach.

Conclusion

Few, if any, Americans escaped the impact of the Depression. As they listened to Franklin D. Roosevelt explain his new policies on the radio, few, if any, were left untouched by the sixteen major pieces of legislation that were enacted between March 8 and July 16, 1933. In the thousands they explained their position in painfully scrawled letters to the White House. Men and women with money deposited in banks and those who had lost their savings, homeowners and the homeless, employers and workers, farm owners and tenants, those working and the jobless—all felt the force of new banking and stock market regulation, wage and price controls, crop destruction, relief checks, and the launching of great new public works.

The Driving Forces Behind the Hundred Days

Who were the driving forces behind this explosion of legislation? Historians have identified very different groups as the key drivers. Some argued it was a business elite in capital-intensive industries anxious to safeguard their market share at the expense of troubling competitors. But others thought it was rabidly antibusiness New Dealers. These men, who had never met a payroll, were imbued with the regulatory zeal of Brandeis and Frankfurter and their lawyer acolytes, the antiprofit motives of Rex Tugwell, or the wage demands of organized labor.

All these groups played some part in the legislation of the Hundred Days, but none of them could be identified as the predominant driving force.

The role businessmen played in the Hundred Days, and their response to the legislation, varied greatly according to size, region, and the industrial or financial sector they represented. There was no monolithic business "interest" and no common business agenda.

Bankers contributed little to the emergency banking legislation—that task fell to holdover Treasury and Federal Reserve officials. But the bankers were responsible for implementing the legislation that rescued so many of their banks. They were happy to see the Reconstruction Finance Corporation, under Houston banker Jesse Jones, underwrite their capital. Nevertheless the larger bankers were powerless to institute a new system of national and branch banking, to stop the separation of investment and commercial banking, or to prevent the establishment of deposit insurance. Men such as the du Ponts, and the auto and petrochemical industries they represented, favored the legalization of beer and the ultimate repeal of Prohibition. They saw these measures as a means of lessening their tax burden and making amends for the government confiscation of business. But most other Hundred Days policies, apart from the Economy Act, they saw as increasing the regulatory burden and, so, their costs.

Some businessmen were undoubtedly enthusiastic about industrial self-regulation under the NRA codes. For example, trade associations in atomistic, excessively competitive industries such as textiles and coal saw the NRA as an opportunity to put into practice the cooperative measures restricting production and stabilizing prices and wages that they had previously tried to implement on a purely voluntary basis. Representatives of some capital-intensive, consumer-durable industries wanted to end destructive competition, which had eliminated most of their welfare capitalism. They were no longer able to provide benefits for their workers, and the consumer purchasing power of the families of their workers had been drastically reduced. But even those groups that sponsored the National Industrial Recovery Act had little interest in the public works program (support for that was left to the construction industry), and they failed to secure government loans that would indemnify business against losses.

More businessmen were uneasy about the NRA. Corporations that already exercised quasi-monopolistic control of their industries, such as automobiles and steel, already largely controlled prices and production: the danger for them was that NRA codes would raise their wage costs and encourage unionization. Many smaller businessmen saw the NRA as strangling their competitive advantage and raising their costs. If such businessmen grudgingly backed the NRA it was only for fear of something worse: the thirty-hour workweek bill or currency inflation.

Yet if many businessmen did not see the NRA as likely to be helpful, they did not share the hostility of power companies and financiers to the whole of the Hundred Days. Businessmen in the South and West favored the New Deal public works investment in their regional infrastructure. They looked forward to assistance from the Reconstruction Finance Corporation, and they welcomed measures to increase agricultural purchasing power, since farmers were important customers. They had no love for the giant utility holding companies that made their power expensive nor for New York bankers who were unresponsive to their capital and credit needs.

The attitude of southern and western businessmen, and indeed farmers, helps explain why some historians see an antibusiness campaign animating the New Deal during the Hundred Days. There is little evidence of a campaign against businessmen or against capitalism. There is plenty of evidence, from all parts of the country, of hostility toward financiers and captains of industry. Given the loss of standing of bankers and utility companies as a result of the Depression, it is perhaps surprising that there was not more of an antibusiness agenda in the summer of 1933.

The lawyers encouraged by Felix Frankfurter to staff government agencies in the Hundred Days were not by and large anticapitalist (although a small number were members of the Communist Party): many came from leading Wall Street law firms and investment houses. They were aware of the betrayal of fiduciary trust by investment bankers and utility companies, and they were anxious that the government should have legal expertise to match the legal teams of the corporations and finance houses. They were suspicious of the pricing policies of the firms they dealt with. They had a lawyer's skepticism of, rather than a businessman's trust in, the good faith of the food processors, for example, to set prices fairly. They expected to have access to the companies' books to check that good faith. They had a rather lofty faith in their ability as disinterested lawyers to act in the national interest. But they were not anticapitalist or antimarket: they aimed instead to get the market to operate in a more open and transparent way.

As an institutional economist, Rexford Tugwell shared this lack of faith in business pricing decisions. But though Tugwell may not have shared the lawyers' faith in a transparent, self-correcting market, his ideas for central planning were never more than academic. His radical ideas had little influence on the Hundred Days, no matter how much he was held up by the right as a bogeyman. Where Tugwell did have influence was alongside Henry Wallace in the Department of Agriculture. Neither Tugwell nor Wallace was an agricultural fundamentalist—interested only in raising farm income in the short term at all costs. In their views on long-term agricultural adjustment—the better use of land, the better adjustment of farmers' production to market conditions—they spoke the language of the agricultural economists in the Bureau of Agricultural Economics and the land-grant colleges. Tugwell may have tossed off ideas on the unsuitability of private proprietorship for agriculture, but these ideas did not affect his policy proposals during the Hundred Days. Wallace, an extremely successful farm businessman himself, could not be accused of antibusiness or anticapitalist ideas in 1933. Indeed, his sense of social justice for farm tenants and for the permanently poor in rural America was largely undeveloped in 1933. What Tugwell and Wallace were arguing for in 1933 was the same control over production and prices for individualistic farmers that organized business exercised in the rest of America.

Nor were the seemingly radical leaders of the Farmers' Holiday Association and the National Farmers Union antibusiness in 1933. They attacked what they saw as the impractical schemes of the intellectuals in Wallace's new policy team, particularly the notion of production control, and they were prepared to take the law into their own hands. But what they wanted was to protect the homestead and the income of the individual farmer, and to do so without any bureaucratic statist apparatus.

If farmers were a major force in the Hundred Days, organized labor certainly was not. The old craft unions of the A. F. of L. could not even dictate the choice of secretary of labor: they accepted the nomination of a female social reformer with an ill grace. They could not deliver on the thirty-hour workweek bill or on wage rates for PWA workers, though building unions were an important lobby for public works spending. Where labor did have some influence was in Senator Robert Wagner's entourage. Wagner had been closely involved in the progressive attempts to stabilize industrial relations in the New York garment trades. In pushing for industrial recovery legislation, Wagner turned to academics and union leaders he had worked with then and to representatives of the United Mine Workers—coal was another industry where labor was anxious to offset the effects of destructive competition on labor standards. But unions simply did not have the strength to drive up wages in the NRA code negotiations as employers feared. Labor was consistently outgunned by business. What the Hundred Days and Section 7a of the Recovery Act did do was raise workers' expectations and spur ambitious union leaders to convey to workers that the government was on their side and might, in the future, protect their organizing drives.

Robert Wagner, alongside Robert La Follette, Jr., of Wisconsin, was a congressional figure who could not be ignored during the Hundred Days and represented a powerful urban liberalism that would increasingly come to define the New Deal and the national Democratic Party for the next forty years. But Wagner and La Follette were the exception rather than the rule. The most influential forces in Congress were rural—the southern Democrats and the western progressives. They represented the interests of farmers, of small-town county seat elites, and of the regional bankers and entrepreneurs. They were not antibusiness or anticapitalist. The western progressives, in particular, were antistatist and antibureaucratic. Some leaders, such as majority leader Senator Joseph Robinson of Arkansas, were conservative allies of the dominant railroad and utility interests in their states. Others, such as Burton K. Wheeler, in Montana, were bitter enemies of the dominant interests in their states (in Wheeler's case, the Anaconda Copper Company). But what they all shared was, first, a fierce determination to rescue the distressed farmers; second, a profound suspicion of great monopolies; and third, a real lack of sympathy for eastern bankers and financial institutions. It was the sentiments of these men that shaped so much of the legislation of the Hundred Days, from the Banking Acts, to farm recovery legislation, to the TVA, to securities legislation. Here was the source of so much of what later historians on the right identified as the antibusiness policies of the Hundred Days.

The Hundred Days also brought to Washington and policy making new forces and new minds. Never before had so many young lawyers come to the capital. Many envisaged a far more interventionist and proactive role for themselves than earlier generations of lawyers had considered. They viewed the law as a creative and adaptive instrument. At a time when not even the notion of a public interest law firm existed, government service gave these lawyers the opportunity to give their social justice aspirations a more tangible form. They were also more intellectually able than their predecessors: as during World War I, government service again became a career option for the best and brightest law school graduates.

From the moment Roosevelt enlisted the services of the Brains Trust in 1932, academics and intellectuals became part and parcel of the federal government to an unprecedented extent. University law schools and Felix Frankfurter were not the only source of academic advice. During the Hundred Days, agriculture was the most obvious place in which in Richard S. Kirkendall's phrase "service intellectuals" played a major role. The Agriculture Department was headed by Wallace and Tugwell, one a statistician and a crop geneticist, the other an economist. The domestic allotment plan had been devised by agricultural economists in the Bureau of Agricultural Economics and in the land-grant colleges. Agricultural economists such as John Black, Howard Tolley, and M. L. Wilson came in to run many of the crop sections of the AAA. But elsewhere, notably at the NRA, the Treasury, the Justice Department, the great works programs, and the regulatory agencies, economists were also given their opportunity. At a time when academic economic orthodoxy was constantly questioned, the New Deal became what William Barber has described as a "laboratory for economic learning."

For the first time, women became a powerful force in the federal government. Roosevelt selected the first woman cabinet officer when he appointed his New York industrial commissioner, Frances Perkins, to be secretary of labor. Perkins was part of a network of female reformers, a generation of college-educated women who had worked in settlement houses and created pressure groups for social reform during the Progressive Era. They were "social feminists": the vote and political participation were means to attain their social justice aims, notably on behalf of women and children. They were distinct, on the one hand, from the feminists who saw an equal rights amendment as the main goal of female political participation and, on the other, from the later generation of women who were professionally trained as social workers. One member of this network of social feminists, Molly Dewson, had been the most persistent voice demanding that Roosevelt appoint Perkins.

Dewson's demand had political purchase in part because the network of female reformers had gained a political foothold in New York as in no other state. Dewson was secretary of the New York Consumers' League, and in 1928 Eleanor Roosevelt sent her to organize Democratic women in the Midwest. Dewson then lobbied for FDR to appoint Perkins to the Industrial Commission post in New York. Impressed by Roosevelt's willingness to do this and to sign unquestioningly a bill to restrict the hours of women shop workers, Dewson organized New York Women for Roosevelt in 1930. As the Depression savaged labor standards, Dewson believed that organizations like the National Consumers' League had only limited utility. Women had to organize politically to elect sympathetic politicians who would legislate to protect those hard-won improvements in working conditions. In 1932 she traveled west to locate women who would support FDR before the convention and then, working very closely with Eleanor Roosevelt, she headed the Women's Division of the Democratic National Campaign Committee. She bypassed the traditional male-dominated political organizations, found local women who were FDR backers, and put them to work. The Women's Division distributed six million rainbow flyers that focused on the issues, rather than party loyalty, which the social feminists believed women should be interested in. Dewson was greatly aided by Louis Howe and tolerated by Jim Farley. If Farley thought that Dewson would disappear after the election, he was mistaken. Instead she was appointed head of the Women's Division of the DNC and on April 27 presented Farley with a list of a hundred leading women whom she expected to get jobs as a reward for their efforts for FDR in 1932. Dewson and her fellow reformers may have been a new breed of "issue-oriented" politicians, as distinct from the traditional male patronage-oriented politicos, notably congressmen, but Dewson was as anxious as any male political leader to secure jobs for her supporters so that they could implement their social-feminist agenda. If Dewson was to be successful in twisting the arm of a reluctant Farley, she would need the backing of her friend Eleanor Roosevelt.

Eleanor Roosevelt dreaded going to the White House. She wondered if she would be able to maintain the independent life she had carved out for herself as a journalist, teacher, and public speaker during the 1920s. She had seen how life in the White House had confined and frustrated even the most strong-willed First Ladies. Her fears were unfounded. She installed her friend the journalist Lorena Hickok in the White House, setting up what has been described as a "competing court." She entertained her own friends and political contacts, kept a formidable program of public engagements, and organized teas. The president's "court," presided over by Missy LeHand, was one of early-evening cocktails, dinner guests who might amuse FDR, and evening poker games and movies.

But Eleanor Roosevelt complemented her husband's political activities. On March 6 she held her first regular press conference. Previous First Ladies had met the press only occasionally. Mrs. Roosevelt intended to meet the press every week. It would be easier to meet them all at once, rather than seeing two or three journalists every now and again. On Hickok's prompting she also wanted to encourage newspapers to send women journalists to cover the White House. The idea, she told the women journalists, was "largely to make an understanding between the White House and the general public. You are the interpreters to the women of the country as to what goes on politically in the legislative national life, and also what the social and personal life is at the White House." So, only women journalists came to the conferences. The first one was so crowded that some of them had to sit on the floor. They became fiercely protective of Mrs. Roosevelt—ensuring that her comments were off the record whenever she seemed likely to stray unwittingly into controversy.

The conferences covered the First Lady's list of engagements, family news about the Roosevelt children, and Mrs. Roosevelt's views on firecrackers, summer holidays, how important it was for women to read newspapers, and in what way they should read them. But these conventional domestic items and the patronizing, didactic advice did not represent either Mrs. Roosevelt's public or her behind-the-scenes role in the Hundred Days. When veterans marched on Washington, as they had in 1932, to demand payment of the bonus, Louis Howe organized a campsite for them at an army base, provided meals for them, and offered them the chance to enlist in the CCC. Howe also asked Mrs. Roosevelt to visit them. She reported back to her press conference that, far from being a threat to law and order, "It was as comfortable as a camp can be, remarkably clean and orderly, grand-looking boys, a fine spirit. There was no kind of disturbance, nothing but the most courteous behavior." Later she reported on visiting destitute Arizona copper miners, a trip organized by her close friend Congresswoman Isabella Greenway, and graphically described their plight.

Mrs. Roosevelt worked closely with Louis Howe and each evening she put a bundle of notes in the night basket by the president's bed for him to read. Each day she swam with him in the newly constructed White House pool. She continued to be his eyes and ears and to be a conduit for, on the whole, progressive political advice. Above all she was a spokesperson for Dewson's patronage demands.

In the long run, women would have more political influence in New Deal Washington than ever before, and would not exercise similar influence again until the 1970s. They did so because the expertise the government needed in the New Deal was in the area of social welfare, where women had disproportionate professional experience. But in the Hundred Days, where the emphasis was on economic recovery and immediate relief, this influence was not yet required. Dewson made little headway with the patronage list, and New Deal legislation largely ignored the plight of women workers. Where women did make progress was not in Washington but in the localities. In FERA, Hopkins turned time and again to women social workers to head up state relief administrations. Only later in 1933 would Dewson get significant patronage plums and put women on the consumer and labor advisory boards of the NRA.

If the Hundred Days largely bypassed women's needs and issues, the period was also overwhelmingly lily white. African Americans were largely onlookers during the Hundred Days. The president had had little to do with African American spokesmen. By contrast, he was comfortable with the southern Democrats who were his congressional leaders. Key members of his White House staff were white southerners, and they held traditional racial attitudes. In 1932, African Americans in northern cities had remained loyal to the Republican Party. While the Roosevelts replaced the white servants in the White House with blacks, and the Fisk Jubilee singers sang at the White House, African American journalists were excluded from both the president's and Mrs. Roosevelt's press conferences. In policy terms, the plight of domestic servants and agricultural laborers did not figure in the legislation of the Hundred Days. Farm-recovery legislation threatened to harm black workers by lessening the demand for tenant farmers and farm laborers. Industrial recovery legislation perpetuated racial differentials in wages under the guise of regional and job differentials. Higher wages encouraged employers to keep whites and fire blacks. State administration of federal relief programs looked likely to maintain existing discrimination against blacks in terms of both eligibility and size of benefits. CCC camps were segregated. In due course, black civil rights would become part of a New Deal liberal agenda. A cabinet officer who championed civil rights such as Harold Ickes would desegregate his Interior

Department and insist on proportionate black employment on PWA projects. Under Harry Hopkins, the relatively nondiscriminatory relief programs in northern cities would secure the switch of allegiance of African American voters in 1934. A newly aware Eleanor Roosevelt would ensure black leaders' access to the president past the southern gatekeepers at the White House. But in the Hundred Days there was little hint of the changes to come that would transform both the Democratic Party and American liberalism.

The Defining Moment

What did the people from such varied backgrounds create in Washington in the summer of 1933? For many Americans it was the defining moment of the twentieth century. But not all approved of what had been defined.

The first generation of New Deal historians came of age in the 1930s. They, and the postwar generation of Democratic politicians who grew up in the Depression, saw the Hundred Days as the turning point for the federal government and the social democratic project. In their eyes, a bold, charismatic president who inspired confidence had replaced an obstinate and unpopular leader who could do nothing to dispel fear. Political paralysis in the face of financial collapse was replaced by political dynamism that rescued the banks and instilled responsibility and discipline in America's financial institutions that lasted for half a century. Before 1933 the federal government had been largely irrelevant to ordinary Americans, except in times of war. During the Hundred Days the federal government took responsibility for the plight of farmers, workers, and the unemployed. The changes started in the Hundred Days served to cement the loyalty of lower-income Americans to the Democratic Party. Ordinary Americans came to trust the federal government. In the Hundred Days the federal government would take responsibility for managing the economy and would later appear to do that with spectacular success after 1945. By 1963, 75 percent of Americans believed that the federal government would "do the right thing." At a time when the social fabric looked likely to disintegrate, the inclusive politics of the Hundred Days and the New Deal engendered a national unity that enabled Americans to marshal national resources to defeat Hitler. In the Hundred Days, according to the most recent account, Roosevelt saved democracy and instituted a "new notion of social obligation."

For Americans who lament the persistence of poverty, the discrepancies of wealth and power in America, and the evils of large American corporations, liberal celebration of the Hundred Days is misplaced. They argue that the Hundred Days was indeed the defining moment for American radicals, but it was a defining moment because it was a great missed opportunity, the one time in the twentieth century when there was a real chance of radical anticapitalist change. American capitalism had an inherent compulsion to overproduce because business would not redistribute its profits into wages sufficient to enable American workers to purchase what American industry produced. Normally, American corporations solved this problem by market expansion overseas. In 1933 they could not: foreign trade had collapsed. In addition, radical farmers and workers demanded change at home, and the financial system had collapsed. Surely no better opportunity existed for a redistribution of wealth and the reordering of American capitalism. Instead, in the Hundred Days, Roosevelt and his advisers rescued corporate capitalism and guaranteed its survival and ever-increasing power. The New Dealers passed up the opportunity to nationalize the banks. They allowed large corporations to fend off challenges from smaller firms and extend their hegemonic control of the economy. Measures to help farmers, workers, and the unemployed were merely palliatives that were sufficient to defuse the threat of disorder but insufficient to disrupt corporate prerogatives.

Economists and economic historians see the Great Depression and the Hundred Days in another light: the defining moment in the twentieth century that "altered the basic rules, institutions and attitudes governing the economy." Americans, previously skeptical of government, accepted an expansion of the federal government and believed that government should get things done when the free market failed. Voters held the government responsible for the overall health of the economy and expected the government, rather than the market, to secure full employment and economic growth. Much of this changed expectation, and much of the growth of the federal government, came later in the New Deal, particularly from 1935, with the new social-insurance programs and a Wagner Act that protected union organization. But the Hundred Days both reflected and contributed to the changed public perception of government and crystallized some of these changes.

Above all, the Hundred Days, according to economic historians, delayed recovery in the United States. New Deal intervention explained why the Depression lasted so long in the United States compared to the rest of the world. Roosevelt did restore confidence in the banks, but the banking reforms perpetuated the status quo. He failed to make possible a system of branch banking, a system that had shielded both Canada and Great Britain from the bank collapses of the 1920s and early 1930s. Deposit insurance was an anticompetitive device that merely safeguarded a system of small banks. The separation of investment and commercial banking simply dried up one more source of the investment that might have brought recovery. Securities reform similarly choked off investment.

The farm programs were futile. It was natural conditions, mainly drought, not the production-control programs of the AAA, that reduced production and raised farm prices.

What the New Deal did right in the Hundred Days was to devalue the dollar (albeit haphazardly and incoherently), which had

the effect of ending the contraction of the money supply that neither the Federal Reserve nor the banks had been able to stem. It
also enabled the United States to escape the "fetters" of the gold
standard. By January 1934 the value of the dollar had declined by
70 percent and from then on, gold flowed into the United States
and boosted the money supply, even though neither federal spending nor the Federal Reserve Board consciously contributed. According to this interpretation, recovery took place temporarily
during the Hundred Days. Speculation, a return of confidence,
and devaluation had an impact. Manufacturing output increased
and unemployment fell by almost a fifth. But then recovery stalled.

What stalled recovery and negated the impact of devaluation
was the National Recovery Administration. The NRA served to
keep prices up and control production: policies "attuned to discourage recovery." Everything the NRA did was "inimical to recovery." Only when the NRA was ended two years later did
business begin to increase production, "released from the shackles
and confusion of the NRA." This eventual recovery, delayed and
far slower than in the rest of the world, left the United States ill
equipped to counter the rise of Nazi Germany.

The analysis of economists and economic historians is dispas-
sionate in some respects but it is underpinned by faith in the market and skepticism about the efficacy of government intervention.
In the 1930s, by contrast, economists who had lived through the
Depression were skeptical about the overarching power of the
market; they trusted government instead. It is not surprising that
the largely critical view of "the defining moment" by economic
historians is grist for the mill of today's historians on the right.
They see a crisis deliberately engineered by Roosevelt in order to
achieve dictatorial powers, which he used to attack business, promote class hatred, and create the modern leviathan, the bloated
bureaucracy of the federal government. Their "defining moment"
of the twentieth century is one with disastrous consequences that
permanently sapped the moral fiber of the American people.

The banking crisis, they believe, was unnecessary. Fear of Roosevelt's radicalism had halted the recovery of the summer of 1932. The collapse of the banks from December 1932 onward was the result of the uncertainty about FDR's economic policies and the publication in January 1933 of the names of banks in receipt of RFC loans. In addition to this petty and vindictive partisan Democratic politics, Roosevelt refused to cooperate with Hoover because he wanted a clean slate in March 1933 on which to sketch his statist plans. Once Roosevelt had reopened the banks, persuaded depositors to put their money back in them, and passed the Economy Act, he should have sent Congress home.

Instead, he used the false analogy of the wartime emergency to drive through measures that relentlessly increased federal power. In his Inaugural Address, Roosevelt likened the crisis of 1933 to a wartime emergency and indicated a willingness to ask for authority "as great as the powers that would be given me if, in fact, we were invaded by a foreign foe." According to historians on the right, Roosevelt exploited this analogy and assumed dictatorial powers. The powers were granted to him by a Congress with a large Democratic majority and a supine Republican opposition. The press, notably columnists such as Walter Lippmann and Mark Sullivan, performed in vain the role that a proper opposition should have played.

As critics on the right see it, the Hundred Days constituted a series of antibusiness measures that cost, rather than created, jobs. The AAA gave radical lawyers access to the books of the major food processors. The NRA raised business costs through higher wages and dramatically increased the bureaucratic regulatory burden on business. The Securities Act scared off investors through its complex, draconian provisions. The TVA set itself up in unfair competition with private utilities and penalized their stockholders. Instead of working for national unity, FDR stoked class hatred and conflict. A gigantic propaganda machine extended federal power and masked FDR's dictatorial ambitions. The relief and public works programs were simply measures designed to bribe the electorate into supporting this dictatorial project. Spending was allocated not in the national interest but in the shameless pursuit of votes and personal power.

Is it possible to cut a swath through these polarized historical interpretations, so weighed down as they are by contemporary political ideology and partisan conflict?

Not even Roosevelt's most ardent defenders would argue that the legislation of the first Hundred Days was coherent and carefully thought out. The cost-slashing imperatives of the Economy Act were countered by the spending impulses of the relief and public works programs. It was unlikely that a balanced budget could easily be obtained in the 1930s given the likely congressional and popular pressure to sustain those spending programs. The desire to rectify the lack of consumer purchasing power was offset by the aim to increase prices, which would be passed on to consumers, and by regressive excise taxes that hit hardest those least able to pay. A long-term desire to promote international trade was countered by immediate nationalist pressures to raise domestic prices and devalue the dollar. What the New Dealers learned was that they were incapable of micromanaging the economy and engineering economic growth. Adjusting wage and price levels by detailed federal government intervention was impossible, outside a war economy, unless there were other engines of economic growth. New Dealers would eventually learn that increasing the money supply and boosting government spending to compensate for the lack of private investment could produce economic growth—without detailed statist, bureaucratic intervention.

It is true that at the end of the Hundred Days the federal government had assumed a responsibility for the economy and the livelihood of ordinary Americans that would be difficult to relinquish subsequently. The Hundred Days, of course, drew on ideas that had been the stuff of intellectual and policy debate since the Progressive Era: the planning ideas of agricultural economists, the use of public works as a countercyclical tool against unemployment, the development of Muscle Shoals, the desires of trade associations to stabilize their industries, the need to regulate the securities market. But in the Hundred Days all these ideas were taken to a quite new level of policy formulation and implementation. Whereas previously farmers and businessmen had been exhorted to reduce their acreage or to maintain prices and wages, they were now paid to cut back crop production and instructed to maintain prices and wages under enforceable codes. Whereas the federal government had once made grudging loans to states for relief, now the federal government made grants for direct unemployment relief. Hoover's loans to states for public works and his infrastructure projects were replaced by a quantum leap in public works spending under the PWA. Proposals to develop Muscle Shoals that had languished in Congress were now given the go-ahead in an ambitious form that their most enthusiastic advocate could not have imagined.

If the New Deal had ended on July 16, 1933, there was much in the New Deal legacy that would have been aborted. Price support loans for farmers, massive work-relief programs, social insurance, the institutionalization of trade unions in the economy, the drive to secure international free trade—all these innovations came later. Other impulses did not last: the drive to cut government spending (despite FDR's reluctance to concede the impossibility of balancing the budget) and the micromanagement of the economy under the NRA. But the footprint of much of the longer-term New Deal legacy could be seen there in 1933. The commitment to sustain farm income would be impossible to abandon. Gigantic work-relief programs were a logical outcome of the Civilian Conservation Corps and FERA. The Wagner Act in 1935 fleshed out the commitment to collective bargaining imperfectly sustained in Section 7a of the National Industrial Recovery Act. FDR had promised Frances Perkins that social insurance would be introduced in the first term. He had promised Cordell Hull that he could seek authority for Reciprocal Trade Agreements in 1934.

The idea of the Hundred Days as a defining moment in twentieth-century America therefore has very considerable purchase. America would have been a very different place over the next fifty years if either Newton Baker or John Nance Garner had received the Democratic nomination in 1932. But critics on the left and the right who lament that defining moment, and who wish that America had gone in a different direction, greatly overestimate the room for maneuver and power that Roosevelt enjoyed in 1933.

When Roosevelt took power on March 4, 1933, many influential Americans doubted the capacity of a democratic government to act decisively enough to save the country. Machine guns guarded government buildings. The newspapers and his audience responded most enthusiastically to Roosevelt's promises in the Inaugural to assume wartime powers if necessary. That sense of emergency certainly made Congress willing to give FDR unprecedented power.

Wartime mobilization was a model that New Dealers turned to in 1933. Agencies such as the War Industries Board served as an explicit model for the NRA. Lawyers and businessmen who had served in Washington during the war returned to government service in 1933. The language of emergency was enshrined in legislation such as the National Industrial Recovery Act, in the hope that it might forestall constitutional challenges. Undoubtedly, the depth of the crisis helped persuade congressmen to back the president. Southern Democrats who held key leadership positions and key chairmanships were prepared to cast aside their traditional limited government and states-rights views because their constituents, notably cotton and tobacco farmers, desperately needed help. Hungry themselves for patronage after twelve years out of the White House, they also needed the jobs that the New Deal agencies would create. The Republicans were divided between traditional conservatives and the western progressives, such as Minority Leader Charles McNary from Oregon, who were glad to see the back of Hoover, and who favored much of the early New Deal program to aid agriculture and build the infrastructure.

But the picture of a president given blanket wartime powers by a complaisant Congress was far from the mark. In the first ten days, Congress passed the Banking Act virtually sight unseen. Republicans offered little challenge to the administration in those early days; indeed the Economy Act passed only with their support. But the granting of broad executive powers in that act—the closest Congress came to giving Roosevelt a blank check—was to cut, not expand, the government. In any case, the wartime model was not of centralized, coercive power and the takeover of private industry; rather it was one of self-regulation and cooperation. While Republicans were prepared to enlist behind the president as behind their commander in chief, in fact they soon started denouncing the powers granted to FDR and the harebrained antibusiness schemes of his advisers. As Clyde Weed has shown, the Republican Party responded to the defeat of 1932 not by moving to the center to embrace the New Deal, as the logic of such a repudiation at the polls might have suggested, but by moving to the right to denounce it.

Congress was not a passive bystander in the Hundred Days. The Farm Act made its way painfully slowly through the House and Senate, despite the impending catastrophe on the land. Roosevelt had to acquiesce to some form of inflationary amendment. Similarly, without the threat of passage of the thirty-hour workweek bill, there would have been no National Industrial Recovery Act. Left to his own devices, FDR would not have launched a massive public works program. But where Congress was prepared to hand over responsibility to Roosevelt was in the implementation of recovery programs. Both the Agricultural Adjustment Act and the National Industrial Recovery Act laid out, but did not resolve, different policy options. Which ones were to be implemented was left to Roosevelt.

For all that Roosevelt might talk of emergency wartime powers, in fact he eschewed, rather than adopted, dictatorial powers.
In a draft for his speech on Sunday, March 5, to the American Legion, a paragraph suggested that he call up an army of veterans
from World War I. He did not use that draft and never showed any
signs of desiring to assume such absolute control.

The emergency limited options rather than opening up possibilities of dictatorial government control. Given the "state capacity" of the federal government Roosevelt inherited, the need for
immediate action dictated the adoption of programs that relied on
voluntarism and consent, not on force and an army of government bureaucrats. The government did not have the capacity simply to act on its own. For speedy action, however, Roosevelt had to
rely not on consent and voluntarism, not on a civil service, but on
bankers, farmers, businessmen, and state governments.

Roosevelt was always hopeful of a quick-fix nonbureaucratic
remedy for the Depression. He never lost his fascination for currency manipulation that would produce the price rises he wanted at
a stroke without micromanaging the economy. For other policy
makers, public works spending that directed contracts toward private construction companies had similar attractions. Farm radicals
regarded currency inflation and the cost-of-production guarantee
as a nonstatist solution to farm problems. The thirty-hour workweek bill and share-the-work schemes had a similar delusive sim-
plicity of their own.

But if more interventionist programs were needed, the need
for speed mandated voluntarism and consent. If the banks were to
be reopened in ten days, the only people who could make an informed judgment on the soundness of individual banks were the
bankers themselves. Millions of individual farmers could not be
ordered to restrict their production: the government simply did
not have the apparatus to enforce such a decree. The domestic allotment plan therefore had to be voluntary and it could not be implemented by a nonexistent army of federal employees. It had to

be put into operation by the farmers themselves and by the county agents of the Extension Service. The federal government alone could not craft a planned industrial recovery program. If NRA codes were to be drafted and enforced, only the businessmen had the information about their industry to draft such codes, which in turn had to be monitored largely by the businessmen themselves. If Hopkins wanted to spend money quickly on unemployment relief, he had to enlist the existing state relief administrations. If Ickes wanted to spend money on public works quickly, he could not establish a direct-labor scheme but had to employ private contractors. He also had to accept that a large percentage of spending would be on defense projects that the War Department and the navy already had in the pipeline. The apparent expansion of federal government power masked a much more limited reality.

The emergency precluded the radical measures of central planning and nationalization. In any case, historians should not assume that there was a politically viable left-wing option. Nothing in the election of 1932 suggested an electoral mandate for more revolutionary change. Ordinary Americans were as likely to turn right as left. The policy alternatives of the most rebellious groups in 1933 such as the midwestern farmers, or of demagogues such as Huey Long, were for antistatist policies that would leave the fundamental structure of agriculture and industry untouched.

The desperate plight of ordinary Americans exposes the wishful thinking that lies behind the criticisms of the economic historians and the lamentations of the right. The immediate prospect of bumper harvests on top of an already glutted market would have destroyed farm income altogether. Angry farmers were taking the law into their own hands to halt foreclosures. Charities and the local and state governments simply could not look after the more than a quarter of the workforce that was out of work. How long would the unemployed who had lost their faith in the beneficence and competence of American businessmen remain fatalistic? It is simply unrealistic to think that the government could stand back and concentrate on cutting spending and securing a controlled international reflation alone. The desperate need of ordinary Americans meant that Roosevelt and Congress did not have the luxury of such a hands-off policy. In any case, there is no compelling evidence that the United States had indeed reached the bottom of an economic slump at which point businessmen would reinvest of their own accord and the economy would naturally revive. The key point about the New Deal in the summer of 1933 was that it gave immediate assistance in cash and kind to those on relief. The farm programs may not have solved the problem of overproduction but they stopped the foreclosures and put money into the hands of southern and midwestern farmers later that year. Drought, rather than crop control, may have raised prices ultimately, but payments under the acreage-reduction contracts and relief payments gave farmers in the drought-stricken regions an income when their crops were bringing in nothing. The NRA may not have created new jobs, but it did stop the relentlessly downward deflationary spiral and sustain labor standards and wages.

In the Hundred Days the New Deal put money into the hands of ordinary Americans without creating a modern bureaucratic leviathan. Despite the proliferation of emergency agencies, the number of people employed by the federal government increased by only 5 percent in 1933. Government spending in 1933 as a percentage of GNP was only 8.3 percent of GNP. Despite the economic emergency, the American state was still a feeble and ramshackle instrument by European standards in July 1933.

Roosevelt gave indispensable assistance to many Americans in the summer of 1933. He instigated a regulatory regime for financial institutions that prevented a repeat of the Great Crash. He made a start on a massive program of investment in the physical infrastructure of the United States. What he had not found in 1933 was the magic key to economic recovery. But in the Hundred Days Roosevelt demonstrated that a democracy need not be paralyzed in the face of economic catastrophe. He inspired a new generation of public servants for whom government service was an honorable, disinterested calling. They would enable the United States to survive the worst depression in the nation's history with its democratic institutions intact and with enough social cohesion and government and productive capacity to fight a successful world war.

Bibliographical Essay

The many general accounts of the New Deal, of course, cover the Hundred Days. It is still essential to start with the classic William E. Leuchtenburg, *Franklin D. Roosevelt and the New Deal, 1933–1940* (New York: Harper and Row, 1963), but of the subsequent accounts, the most fresh and distinguished is David Kennedy, *Freedom from Fear: The American People in Depression and War, 1929–1945* (Oxford: Oxford University Press, 1999). Similarly, the many biographies of Roosevelt have things to say about the Hundred Days. My skepticism about the utility of the never-ending supply of biographies of FDR is summed up in "The New Deal Without FDR: What Biographies of Roosevelt Cannot Tell Us," in T.C.W. Blanning and David Cannadine, eds., *History and Biography* (Cambridge: Cambridge University Press, 1996), 243–65. The multivolume biographies—by Frank Freidel, *Franklin D. Roosevelt*, vols. 1–3 (Boston: Little, Brown, 1952, 1954, 1956); and Geoffrey C. Ward, *Before the Trumpet: Young Franklin Roosevelt 1882–1905* (New York: Harper, 1985), and *A First-Class Temperament: The Emergence of Franklin Roosevelt* (New York: HarperPerennial, 1989), are indispensable for an understanding of FDR before 1932. To my mind, easily the most analytical biographical study of Roosevelt, and the most helpful for any student of the New Deal, is Patrick J. Maney, *The Roosevelt Presence: A Biography of Franklin Delano Roosevelt* (Toronto: Twayne Publishers, 1992).

Anyone writing on the Hundred Days is indebted to the late Frank Freidel's fourth volume on Roosevelt, *Launching the New Deal* (New York: Little, Brown, 1973), and to the unduly neglected James E. Sargent, *Roosevelt and the Hundred Days: The Struggle for the Early New Deal* (New York: Garland, 1981), a meticulous study that, among its many virtues, reasserts the importance of Lewis W. Douglas. See also Kenneth S. Davis, *FDR: The New Deal Years, 1933–1937* (New York: Random House, 1986). Jonathan Alter has written a superb, vivid study, *The Defining Moment: FDR's Hundred Days and the Triumph of Hope* (New York: Simon and Schuster, 2006). Alter captures particularly well the sense of crisis in spring 1933 and the very powerful calls for some sort of dictatorship. He compares FDR's triumph over his own physical paralysis to his triumph over the national paralysis of

March 1933. Alter pays more attention than most historians to the failed assassination attempt on February 15 and the positive national response to FDR's calmness in the face of danger. He is less interested in the specifics of the legislation of the Hundred Days, though, which occupy only about 10 percent of the book.

INTRODUCTION

William E. Leuchtenburg, *In the Shadow of FDR: From Harry Truman to Bill Clinton* (Ithaca, N.Y.: Cornell University Press, 1993), shows how Democratic presidents and candidates have struggled since 1945 to live up to the reputation of a charismatic leader who was so successful with both the electorate and, for a time, Congress. The liberal celebratory accounts of the New Deal were challenged in the 1960s by New Left historians, but their provocative essays never led to a substantial overview to match the narratives by Arthur M. Schlesinger, Jr., or William E. Leuchtenburg. The closest to a general "corporate liberal" interpretation of the New Deal did not appear until 1994, with Colin Gordon's *New Deals: Business, Labor, and Politics, 1920–1935* (Cambridge: Cambridge Univesity Press, 1994). My own book in 1990, *The New Deal: The Depression Years, 1933–1940* (reprinted Chicago: Ivan Dee, 2002), reflected the interpretations of the 1970s and 1980s, which stressed the limitations and constraints within which the New Deal operated. For the view that the New Deal constituted a decisive "wrong turn" in American history, see Robert Higgs, *Crisis and Leviathan: Critical Episodes in the Growth of American Government* (New York: Oxford University Press, 1989); Gary Dean Best, *Pride, Prejudice, and Politics: Roosevelt Versus Recovery, 1933–1938* (New York: Praeger, 1990); and Jim Powell, *FDR's Folly: How Roosevelt and His New Deal Prolonged the Great Depression* (New York: Three Rivers Press, 2004). The views of economic historians can be traced in Michael Bordo, Claudia Goldin, and Eugene N. White, eds., *The Defining Moment: The Great Depression and the American Economy in the Twentieth Century* (Chicago: University of Chicago Press, 1997), and in Gene Smiley, *Rethinking the Great Depression* (Chicago: Ivan Dee, 2002). Alonzo Hamby brings together a number of these interpretations in *For the Survival of Democracy: Franklin Roosevelt and the World Crisis of the 1930s* (New York: Free Press, 2004), which seeks to explain why the Depression lasted longer in the United States than in Europe. Jordan Schwarz, *The New Dealers: Power Politics in the Age of Roosevelt* (New York: Free Press, 1994), is the key book that stresses the importance of the New Deal investment in infrastructure.

1. THE PROBLEM AND THE PLAYERS

For an excellent introduction to the 1920s boom and the Depression, see Peter Fearon, *War, Prosperity, and Depression: The U.S. Economy, 1917–1945* (Lawrence: University Press of Kansas, 1987). Michael Bernstein, *The Great Depression: Delayed Recovery and Economic Change in America, 1929–1939* (Cambridge: Cambridge University Press, 1987), finds the explanation for the long-lasting nature of the American Depression in the relatively fledgling state of successful new industries at the time of the financial crisis. Barry Eichengreen, *Golden Fetters: The Gold Standard and the Great Depression, 1919–1939* (New York: Oxford University Press, 1992), shows how the gold standard in the interwar years exported financial instability and retarded recovery. Gene Smiley's *Rethinking the Great Depression* places the blame on national efforts to maintain the gold standard and on the interventionist policies of both Hoover and Roosevelt. The Depression and the "unbearably slow" recovery in the United States were, according to Smiley, "tragic testimony to government interference in market economies."

The best single-volume biography of Hoover remains David Burner's *Herbert Hoover: A Public Life* (New York: Knopf, 1979). The other biographies that eschew the old notion of an uncaring, conservative Hoover include John Hoff Wilson, *Herbert Hoover: Forgotten Progressive* (Boston: Little, Brown, 1975), and Martin L. Fausold, *The Presidency of Herbert C. Hoover* (Lawrence: University Press of Kansas, 1985). Hoover's ideas on how to foster economic growth and tackle unemployment are shrewdly explored in William J. Barber, *From New Era to New Deal: Herbert Hoover, the Economists, and American Economic Policy, 1921–1933* (Cambridge: Cambridge University Press, 1985), and Udo Sautter, *Three Cheers for the Unemployed: Government and Unemployment Before the New Deal* (New York: Cambridge University Press, 1991). The two authoritative accounts of key Hoover policies are David E. Hamilton, *From New Day to New Deal: American Farm Policy from Hoover to Roosevelt, 1928–1933* (Chapel Hill: University of North Carolina Press, 1991), and James Stuart Olson, *Herbert Hoover and the Reconstruction Finance Corporation, 1931–1933* (Ames: Iowa State University Press, 1977).

For Roosevelt's background and development, see Geoffrey C. Ward, *A First-Class Temperament.* For the Brains Trusters, see Rex Tugwell's own account, *The Brains Trust* (New York: Viking Press, 1968), Jordan A. Schwarz, *Liberal: Adolf A. Berle and the Vision of an American Era* (New York: Free Press, 1987), and Elliot Rosen, *Hoover, Roosevelt, and the Brains Trust: From Depression to New Deal* (New York: Columbia University Press, 1977). Rosen's book also offers—together with Douglas B. Craig, *After Wilson: The Struggle for the Democratic Party, 1920–1934* (Chapel Hill: University of North Carolina Press, 1992)—an excellent account of the campaign to stop Roosevelt from winning the nomination in 1932.

2. TEN DAYS THAT OPENED THE BANKS

Susan Estabrook Kennedy, *The Banking Crisis of 1933* (Lexington: University Press of Kentucky, 1933), is the standard narrative of the banking crisis. James S. Olson, *Saving Capitalism: The Reconstruction Finance Corporation and the New Deal, 1933–1940* (Princeton, N.J.: Princeton University Press, 1988), provides an excellent account of its development. Herbert Feis, *1933: Characters in Crisis* (Boston: Little, Brown, 1966), and the oral history interviews at Columbia University by Walter Wyatt and Eugene Meyer illuminate the failure of Hoover's last-ditch efforts and the frantic negotiations between the incoming Roosevelt team and the Treasury holdovers. Elliot Rosen's *Hoover, Roosevelt* and Raymond Moley's *The First New Deal* (New York: Harcourt Brace and World, 1966) stress the contribution of the Republican holdovers and its importance in saving capitalism. Elliot A. Rosen, *Roosevelt, the Great Depression, and the Economics of Recovery* (Charlottesville: University of Virginia Press, 2005), stresses the disingenuous, self-serving, and flawed nature of Hoover's efforts to involve FDR in decision making before March 4. Richard Lowitt, *Bronson M. Cutting: Progressive Politician* (Albuquerque: University of New Mexico Press, 1992), and Patrick J. Maney, *Young Bob La Follette: A Biography of Robert La Follette, Jr., 1895–1953* (Columbia: University of Missouri Press, 1978), show the limited nature of the "nationalization" alternative in March 1933. For Hiram Johnson's approval of Roosevelt's performance, see Richard Coke Lower, *A Bloc of One: The Political Career of Hiram W. Johnson* (Stanford, Calif.: Stanford University Press, 1993).

For Roosevelt's first press conference and his first fireside chat, see Graham J. White, *FDR and the Press* (Chicago: University of Chicago Press, 1979), Betty Houchin Winfield, *FDR and the News Media* (Urbana: University of Illinois Press, 1990), Russell D. Buhite and David W. Levy, *FDR's Fireside Chats* (Norman: University of Oklahoma Press, 1992), and Jonathan Daniels, ed., *Complete Presidential Press Conferences of Franklin Roosevelt, 1933–1945* (New York: Da Capo, 1973).

3. FIRST PRIORITIES

For the history of budget deficits in the United States, see Iwan W. Morgan, *Deficit Government: Taxing and Spending in Modern America* (Chicago: I. R. Dee, 1995), and James D. Savage, *Balanced Budgets and American Politics* (Ithaca, N.Y.: Cornell University Press, 1988). For taxpayers' protests see David Beito, *Taxpayers in Revolt: Tax Resistance During the Great Depression* (Chapel Hill: University of North Carolina Press, 1989); for veterans, see Nancy Beck Young's biography of their champion, Wright Patman, *Wright Patman: Populism, Liberalism and the American Dream* (Dallas: Southern Methodist University Press, 2000). For taxation, see W. Eliott Brownlee, *Federal Taxation in America: A Short History* (Cambridge, UK: Cambridge University Press, 2004), and Mark Leff, *The Limits of Symbolic Reform: The New Deal and Taxation, 1933–1939* (Cambridge, UK: Cambridge University Press, 1984). For the repeal of Prohibition, see Donald E. Kyvig, *Repealing National Prohibition* (Chicago: University of Chicago Press, 1979). Robert Paul Browder and Thomas G. Smith, *Independent: A Biography of Lewis W. Douglas* (New York: Alfred A. Knopf, 1986), provides a compelling portrait of Roosevelt's articulate and charming budget director, and Julian E. Zelizer shows how important fiscal conservatism was to Roosevelt's overall project in "The Forgotten Legacy of the New Deal: Fiscal Conservatism and the Roosevelt Administration, 1933–1938," *Presidential Studies Quarterly* 30 (2000): 331–58.

John A. Salmond's *The Civilian Conservation Corps and the New Deal, 1933–1942* (Durham, N.C.: Duke University Press, 1965) remains the standard book on the CCC. For FDR and conservation, see Edgar B. Nixon, *Franklin D. Roosevelt and Conservation, 1911–1945* (Manchester, N.H.: Ayer Co. Publishing, 1972). Howard Lange's memoir of the first days of the CCC is *The CCC: A Humanitarian Endeavor During the Great Depression* (New York: Vantage Press, 1984).

There are two substantial biographies of Harry Hopkins: June Hopkins, *Harry Hopkins: Sudden Hero, Brash Reformer* (New York: St. Martin's Press, 1999), and George McJimsey, *Harry Hopkins: Ally of the Poor, Defender of Democracy* (Cambridge, Mass.: Harvard University Press, 1987). William W. Bremer places Hopkins in the essential context of a network of New York social workers in *Depression Winters: New York Social Workers and the New Deal* (Philadelphia: Temple University Press, 1984). William R. Brock, *Welfare, Democracy and the New Deal* (Cambridge: Cambridge University Press, 1988), and Jeff Singleton, *The American Dole: Unemployment Relief and the Welfare State in the Great Depression* (Westport, Conn.: Greenwood, 2000), illustrate the continuities and changes in relief policies and their impact on the local level. Of the more recent descriptions of local relief provision in March 1933, the two most insightful are Jo Ann E. Argersinger, *Toward a New Deal in Baltimore: People and Governance in the Great Depression* (Chapel Hill: University of North Carolina Press, 1988), and Peter Fearon, *Kansas in the Great Depression: Work Relief, Dole, and Rehabilitation* (Columbia: University of Missouri Press, 1987).

David Danbom, *Born in the Country: A History of Rural America*, 2nd ed. (Baltimore: Johns Hopkins University Press, 2006), explains the "best of times and the worst of times" for American farmers between the wars. Older studies of farm issues in 1933 remain important. Van L. Perkins wrote the standard account of the development of the Agricultural Adjustment Administration in 1933 in *Crisis in Agriculture: The Agricultural Adjustment Administration and the New Deal, 1933* (Berkeley: University of California Press, 1969). Richard S. Kirkendall, *Social Scientists and Farm Politics in the Age of Roosevelt* (Columbia: University of Missouri Press, 1967), and William D. Rowley, *M. L. Wilson and the Campaign for the Domestic Allotment* (Lincoln: University of Nebraska Press, 1971), show how agricultural economists shaped New Deal farm policy, exploiting the fact that the federal government, through the Bureau of Agricultural Economics and the Extension Service, had the "state capacity" lacking in most other areas of government. John L. Shover, *Cornbelt Rebellion: The Farmers' Holiday Association* (Urbana: University of Illinois Press, 1965), and Lowell K. Dyson, *Red Radicalism: The Communist Party and American Farmers* (Lincoln: University of Nebraska Press, 1982), describe the context of radical grassroots protest that formed the backdrop for the farm legislation. More recently, David Hamilton, *From New Day to New Deal*, brilliantly delineates the continuities of voluntarism in the Hoover and FDR farm policies. There are two major biographies of Henry Wallace: Graham J. White and John Maze, *Henry Wallace: His Search for a New World Order* (Chapel Hill: University of North Carolina Press, 1995), and John C. Culver and John C. Hyde, *American Dreamer:*

The Life and Times of Henry Wallace (New York: Norton, 2000). Peter Fearon, *Kansas in the Great Depression,* and Keith J. Volanto, *Texas, Cotton, and the New Deal* (College Station: Texas A&M University Press, 2005), show how confusing and slow the New Deal farm program could be for farmers in 1933.

4. INDUSTRIAL RECOVERY: THE BELATED PRIORITY

The background of proposals for public works spending can be found in Udo Sautter's *Three Cheers for the Unemployed.* For Robert Wagner's ideas about both public works and industrial codes, see Joseph Huthmacher, *Senator Robert F. Wagner and the Rise of Urban Liberalism* (New York: Atheneum, 1971). Stanley Vittoz examines the variety of start-up and share-the-work recovery proposals in "The Economic Foundations of Industrial Politics in the United States and the Emerging Structural Theory of the State in Capitalist Society: The Case of New Deal Labor Policy," *Amerikastudien* 27 (1982): 369–74. Nelson Lloyd Dawson, *Louis D. Brandeis, Felix Frankfurter and the New Deal* (Hamden, Conn.: Archon, 1980), and Michael Parrish, *Felix Frankfurter and His Times: The Reform Years* (New York: The Free Press, 1982), lay out the antimonopoly alternatives in their more sophisticated forms. The classic delineation of the conflicting ideas about how to treat concentrations of economic power and secure recovery that lay behind the NRA is Ellis W. Hawley, *The New Deal and the Problem of Monopoly* (Princeton, N.J.: Princeton University Press, 1966). Robert Himmelberg, *The Origins of the National Recovery Administration: Business, Government and the Trade Association Issue* (New York: Fordham University Press, 1976), traces the role of trade association leaders. Colin Gordon, *New Deals,* stresses the promotion of the NRA by anticompetitive business leaders. Elliot A. Rosen, *Roosevelt, the Great Depression, and the Economics of Recovery,* convincingly demonstrates the lack of business enthusiasm for the Recovery Act. John Kennedy Ohl, *Hugh Johnson and the New Deal* (DeKalb: Northern Illinois University Press, 1985), chronicles the activities of the NRA administrator.

We now have a first-rate biography of Harold Ickes, in Jeanne Nienaber Clarke, *Roosevelt's Warrior: Harold L. Ickes and the New Deal* (Baltimore: Johns Hopkins University Press, 1996), and a brilliant study of the origins and launching of the Public Works Administration, Jason Scott Smith, *Building New Deal Liberalism: The Political Economy of Public Works, 1933–1956* (Cambridge: Cambridge University Press, 2006).

5. THE PROGRESSIVE IMPULSE

We are fortunate to have fine biographies of three of the critical individuals in the creation of the TVA and its early days: Richard Lowitt, *George W. Norris: The Persistence of a Progressive, 1913–1933* (Urbana: University of Illinois Press, 1971), Roy Talbert, Jr., *FDR's Utopian: Arthur Morgan of the TVA* (Jackson: University

Press of Mississippi, 1987), Stephen M. Neuse, *David E. Lilienthal: The Journey of an American Liberal* (Knoxville: University of Tennessee Press, 1996). For Lilienthal's own account, see David E. Lilienthal, *The Journals of David E. Lilienthal*, vol. 1, *The TVA Years, 1939–1945* (New York: Harper and Row, 1964), 24–39. Jordan A. Schwarz's *The New Dealers* traces the implications of Lilienthal's commitment to infrastructure development at home and overseas. For the wider history of the TVA, see Richard Lowitt, "The TVA, 1933–1945," in Edwin C. Hargrove and Paul K. Conkin, eds., *TVA: Fifty Years of Grass-roots Democracy* (Urbana: University of Illinois, 1983), and Thomas K. McGraw, *TVA and the Power Fight, 1933–1939* (Philadelphia: J. B. Lippincott, 1971). For a key congressional southern supporter who came around to support the TVA, see Virginia Hamilton, *Lister Hill: Statesman from the South* (Chapel Hill: University of North Carolina Press, 1987).

Michael E. Parrish, *Securities Regulation and the New Deal* (New Haven, Conn.: Yale University Press, 1970), provides the definitive account of the passage of the 1933 Truth in Securities legislation. For the background of the Pecora exposé of stock market abuses, see Donald Ritchie, "The Pecora Wall Street Exposé 1934," in Arthur Schlesinger, Jr., and Roger Burns, eds., *Congress Investigates: A Documentary History, 1792–1974*, vol. 4 (New York: Chelsea House Publishers, 1975). For the role of Frankfurter and the background of his young followers, Cohen, Corcoran, and Landis, see Michael Parrish, *Felix Frankfurter and His Times: The Reform Years* (New York: The Free Press, 1982), Joseph Lash, *From the Diaries of Felix Frankfurter* (New York: Norton, 1975), Joseph P. Lash, *Dealers and Dreamers: A New Look at the New Deal* (New York: Doubleday, 1988), William Lasser, *Benjamin V. Cohen: Architect of the New Deal* (New Haven, Conn.: Yale University Press, 2002), Donald A. Ritchie, *James M. Landis: Dean of the Regulators* (Cambridge, Mass.: Harvard University Press, 1980), and Donald McKean, *Peddling Influence: Thomas "Tommy the Cork" Corcoran and the Birth of Modern Lobbying* (New York: Steerforth, 2005). For Sam Rayburn, see D. B. Hardeman and Donald C. Bacon, *Rayburn: A Biography* (Austin: Texas Monthly Press, 1987).

6. THE INTERNATIONAL OPTION

I have relied heavily on Patricia Clavin's important work on the London conference: Patricia Clavin, "The Fetishes of So-Called International Bankers: Central Bank Cooperation for the World Economic Conference, 1932–1935," *Comparative European History* 1 (1992): 281–311, and Patricia Clavin, *The Failure of Economic Diplomacy: Britain, Germany, France, and the United States, 1931–36* (Basingstoke, UK: Macmillan, 1996). James P. Warburg provides an agonized account of the negotiations leading up to the conference and the conference itself in his diary, which is part of his Oral History interview at the Columbia University Oral History collection. Robert Paul Browder and Thomas G. Smith, *Independent*, detail Lewis Douglas's hopes for the London conference, and Herbert Feis, *1933*, provides his viewpoint from the State Department. Thomas Ferguson's identification of internationalist-oriented businessmen is in Steve Fraser and Gary Gerstle, *The Rise and Fall of the New Deal Order, 1930–1980* (Princeton, N.J.: Princeton University Press, 1989). Charles P. Kindleberger's analysis that London merely confirmed America's refusal to play the constructive role of lender of last resort is in his *The World in Depression, 1929–1939* (Berkeley: University of California Press, 1975). Barry Eichengreen's skepticism of a gold standard settlement is in his *Golden Fetters.* Elliot A. Rosen, *Roosevelt, the Great Depression, and the Economics of Recovery,* shows that Roosevelt's decision to jettison the conference was not cavalier and ill informed but rather reflected inflationary advice from respectable banking sources. Rosen rightly points out that the British were disingenuous in blaming the Americans for the conference's failure. The British never had any intention of accepting a realistic stabilization proposal that would jeopardize the competitive advantages given them by their devaluation and by the tariff wall created by their imperial preference scheme. Michael A. Butler, in *Cautious Visionary: Cordell Hull and Trade Reform, 1933–1937* (Kent, Ohio: Kent State University Press, 1998), takes Cordell Hull seriously and shows how he carried forward his ideas doggedly after 1933.

CONCLUSION

The emphasis on the antibusiness thrust of the Hundred Days is found remorselessly in Gary Dean Best, *Pride, Prejudice and Politics,* and Jim Powell, *FDR's Folly.*

For the southern and western agrarian thrust of early New Deal legislation see Elisabeth Sanders, *Roots of Reform: Farmers, Workers, and the American State, 1877–1917* (Chicago: University of Chicago Press, 1999).

For the role of women in the Hundred Days, see Susan Ware's biography of Molly Dewson, *Partner and I: Molly Dewson, Feminism, and New Deal Politics* (New Haven, Conn.: Yale University Press, 1987), and her analysis of the female network of social reformers, *Beyond Suffrage: Women in the New Deal* (Cambridge, Mass.: Harvard University Press, 1981). Blanche Wiesen Cook details Eleanor Roosevelt's fears of going to Washington and her achievements in *Eleanor Roosevelt,* vols. 1 and 2 (London: Bloomsbury, 1993, 2000). Maurine Beasley traces the development of Mrs. Roosevelt's press conferences in her edition *The White House Press Conferences of Eleanor Roosevelt* (New York: Garland Publishing, 1983).

For lawyers and their role as New Dealers, see Joseph Lash, *Dealers and Dreamers,* and Peter Irons, *New Deal Lawyers* (Princeton, N.J.: Princeton University Press, 1982).

For the lack of impact of labor in 1933, see Robert Zeiger, *American Workers, American Unions, 1920–1985* (Baltimore: Johns Hopkins University Press, 1994).

For the negligible interest in African Americans among political leaders in Washington in 1933, see Raymond Wolters, *Negroes and the Great Depression: The Problem of Economic Recovery* (Westport, Conn.: Greenwood, 1970), and Nancy

Weiss, *Farewell to the Party of Lincoln: Black Politics in the Age of FDR* (Princeton, N.J.: Princeton University Press, 1983).

The indispensable study of Congress in 1933 is James T. Patterson, *Congressional Conservatism and the New Deal: The Growth of the Conservative Coalition in Congress, 1933–1939* (Lexington: University Press of Kentucky, 1967), which shows why influential southern Democrats were mostly prepared to support the New Deal in the Hundred Days. Clyde Weed, *Nemesis of Reform: The Republican Party During the New Deal* (New York: Columbia University Press, 1994), chronicles the initial Republican support of emergency measures but also the forces that would lead the GOP to the right. Steve Neal, by contrast, shows how the minority leader Charles McNary was enthusiastic about almost all aspects of the Hundred Days legislation, in *McNary of Oregon: A Political Biography* (Portland: Oregon Historical Society, 1985). Ronald Feinman, *Twilight of Progressivism: The Western Republican Senators and the New Deal* (Baltimore: Johns Hopkins University Press, 1981), demonstrates the support of western progressives for the New Deal before their suspicions of state power and bureaucracy took precedence. Sean Savage, *Franklin D. Roosevelt as Party Leader, 1932–1945* (Lexington: University Press of Kentucky, 1991), explores the range of FDR's political skills. Daniel M. Scroop, *"Mr. Democrat": Jim Farley, the New Deal, and the Making of Modern American Politics* (Ann Arbor: University of Michigan Press, 2006), shows how Farley handled patronage in the Hundred Days and challenges the conventional picture that Farley was unsympathetic to the emergence of new groups in Democratic liberal politics.

Acknowledgments

Eric Foner and the late Arthur Wang first commissioned me to write this book. Like so many historians I owed much to Arthur's encouragement, support, enthusiasm, and patience. Eric and Thomas LeBien showed remarkable faith in the author and have seen this project through to its conclusion. Liz Maples has overseen the final production meticulously. Ann Holton and Sophie King prepared the manuscript with great skill and care.

This work relies exclusively on the scholarship of others. Readers will recognize my particular debts to David Beito, Robert Paul Browder and Thomas G. Smith, Patricia Clavin, Peter Fearon, the late Frank Freidel, Colin Gordon, David Hamilton, Dick Lowitt, Pat Maney, Iwan Morgan, James S. Olson, Michael E. Parrish, Donald A. Ritchie, Eliot A. Rosen, James E. Sargent, Udo Sautter, the late Jordan Schwarz, Jason Scott Smith, Roy Tolbert, Jr., and Graham White. I have been fortunate to get to know many of these scholars personally, but friends or not, I hope I have done justice to their work. The work of my former student Jon Herbert, of Keele University, on presidential transitions has been indispensable. I am solely responsible, of course, for any errors and misinterpretations in the text.

Kees Van Minnen and the staff of the Roosevelt Study Center at Middelburg have been gracious hosts and supporters for twenty years.

My family has endured the move to Cambridge and to different jobs while this book was being written. Nick and Chris have been cheerful skeptics about their father's putative writing deadlines. Their friendship has been unmatched. Ruth has been the rock on which my life has been based. Without her encouragement and editorial improvements, as well as her sacrifices, love, and support, this book would not have been written.

The book is dedicated to three scholars whose work first put me on the trail of American history forty years ago. For more than thirty years they have also been true friends to a British interloper.

Index